Numerology for Healing

Self Development Guide to Master Your Destiny and Spiritual Growth

(Discover Love and Master Fortune Telling and Better Predict Life Events)

Annemarie Virtue

Published by Rob Miles

© **Annemarie Virtue**

All Rights Reserved

Numerology for Healing: Self Development Guide to Master Your Destiny and Spiritual Growth (Discover Love and Master Fortune Telling and Better Predict Life Events)

ISBN 978-1-989990-44-5

All rights reserved. No part of this guide may be reproduced in any form without permission in writing from the publisher except in the case of brief quotations embodied in critical articles or reviews.

Legal & Disclaimer

The information contained in this book is not designed to replace or take the place of any form of medicine or professional medical advice. The information in this book has been provided for educational and entertainment purposes only.

The information contained in this book has been compiled from sources deemed reliable, and it is accurate to the best of the Author's knowledge; however, the Author cannot guarantee its accuracy and validity and cannot be held liable for any errors or omissions. Changes are periodically made to this book. You must consult your doctor or get professional medical advice before using any of the suggested remedies, techniques, or information in this book.

Upon using the information contained in this book, you agree to hold harmless the Author from and against any damages, costs, and expenses, including any legal fees potentially resulting from the application of any of the information provided by this guide. This disclaimer applies to any damages or injury caused by the use and application, whether directly or indirectly, of any advice or information presented, whether for breach of contract, tort, negligence, personal injury, criminal intent, or under any other cause of action.

You agree to accept all risks of using the information presented inside this book. You need to consult a professional medical practitioner in order to ensure you are both able and healthy enough to participate in this program.

Table of Contents

INTRODUCTION 1

CHAPTER 1: WHAT'S THE NUMEROLOGY CHART? 4

CHAPTER 2: INDEPENDENCE AND THE ENTREPRENEUR OF MANY COLORS 26

CHAPTER 3: SUCCESS NUMBERS AND PRACTICE 31

CHAPTER 4: UNDERSTANDING THE POWER OF THE SYMBOLS 48

CHAPTER 5: THE PURPOSE OF NUMBERS 60

CHAPTER 6: INTRO TO NUMEROLOGY 68

CHAPTER 7: THE MEANING OF MASTER NUMBERS 72

CHAPTER 8: MASTER NUMBERS 79

CHAPTER 9: IF YOU BORN ON THE 4. (FOURTH) OR 13TH (THIRTEEN), OR 22ND (TWENTY SECOND) OR 31ST (THIRTY FIRST) OF ANY MONTH THAN KINDLY READ THE FOLLOWING: 109

CHAPTER 10: COMPARISONS TO ASTROLOGY 126

CHAPTER 11: SOUL NUMBER 130

CHAPTER 12: PERSONAL DAY 137

CHAPTER 13: MASTER NUMBERS 143

CHAPTER 14: VIRGO'S COSMIC CLOCK 146

CHAPTER 15: HOW TO FIND YOUR MOST COMPATIBLE/SOCIAL/ BUSINESS/ LOVE/SEX PARTNER FOR LIFE PATH NUMBER.. 1 - 9 162

CHAPTER 16: PARENTING TRAITS ON BASIS OF NUMBERS 170

CHAPTER 17: ACE OF WANDS 174

CHAPTER 18: PERSONALITY NUMBER 193

CONCLUSION 202

Introduction

Similar to astrology; numerology is also one of the alternative belief systems which is closely related to planets and we can predict readings for personal life, career, life partner, business, travel, vastu etc. Also this will be extended to the monthly, yearly or life time predictions for anyone or anything.

The prediction of future with the help of numbers, which are from Date of Birth, Name &

Signature. Numerology deals with the practical application of the laws of mathematics &

astrology to the material existence.

It is not only like astrology and stops with planetary positions and predictions; but more than astrology by doing miracle with naming the baby or elderly people or organization or business or place etc. The basic vibration comes from the date in which we born, then the sum of date/month/year — each digit and finally the alphabets we use in our name along with the signature. This attracts a specific universal (cosmic) energy depending on the numbers in and around us and our mind; how it remembers and chants or writes our name every day.

Numerology also deals with the nine major planets — Sun, Moon, Jupiter, Uranus (Similar to Ragu), Mercury, Venus, Neptune (Similar to Ketu), Saturn and Mars and their characteristic features. Each one of these nine planets is assigned numbers ranging from 1

to 9, depending on which planet vibrates to a particular number. These nine planets influence the human life in a substantial way.

After birth, the individual starts radiating the vibrations of that number or planet by which he/she is governed. All the characteristics of this individual, ranging from his thinking, reasoning, emotions, philosophy, desires, aversions, health, career, etc. are all dominated by these numbers or their corresponding planets.

When this number is in harmony/ synchronize with the number of any other person, he will experience a harmonious relationship with that person. According to the numerology, only a name and number rule a person. He/ She will encounter opportunities and difficulties in life according to the influence of numbers.

Chapter 1: What's The Numerology Chart?

Numerology is the science of number meanings or vibration. Just like Astrology, Numerology has a birth chart. This book will guide you in finding the numbers in your full Numerology chart using your birth name and birth date.

A full Numerology chart consists of six numbers, three from your name and three from your birthday. This complete chart will describe how you are as a person, how you express yourself, what career path you should take, your likes and dislikes, and other insights into your complete being.

There are other numbers that Numerology takes into account like pinnacle numbers, challenge numbers, karmic lessons, hidden passions, cornerstone numbers, and more. For the sake of this article, we will focus on your 6 core numbers deriving from your name and birth date.

Numerology has what are called Master Numbers and these are any repeating digit numbers (eg.11, 22, 33). Master Numbers are normally NOT reduced to a single digit. However, I suggest you know the meaning of 1-9 before dealing with double digits. Check out the Master Numbers in Numerology article for a better understanding of these powerful numbers.

What You Need for Numerology Charts

Before getting started on a numerology chart, you'll need to have paper and pen handy and be prepared to do some math. As you work, keep the following in mind.

Your Birth Name and Current Name

Use the full name on your birth certificate and the name you are currently using. For example, if you were born Jane Alexis Smith, but you are now Jane Alexis Jones, you'll use each name to calculate different name numerology numbers.

For the calculations below, you'll focus only on your given name at birth.

A Letter Value Numerology Chart

You also need to know the value of each letter to calculate your chart. Different types of numerology have different charts. The chart below is Pythagorean numerology, but there is a different chart for Chaldean numerology.

Pythagorean Numerology

1	2	3	4	5	6	7	8	9
A	B	C	D	E	F	G	H	I
J	K	L	M	N	O	P	Q	R
S	T	U	V	W	X	Y	Z	

Decide Whether Y Is a Vowel or Consonant

Y is always considered a consonant in Pythagorean numerology unless it sounds like a vowel. Then you calculate it as a vowel instead. For example, if your birth name is Candy, the Y has a vowel sound (ee), so you calculate it as a vowel.

Otherwise, such as in the name Young, it is a consonant.

Your Date of Birth

You'll also need your date of birth as mm/dd/yyyy; for example, for December 14, 1969, you would need the numbers 12 (mm), 14 (dd), and 1969 (yyyy).

Constructing the Core Numbers of Numerology Chart

When you begin your calculations, take your time and make sure you're adding numbers correctlyso you don't have to go back and recalculate.

1	2	3	4	5	6	7	8	9
A	B	C	D	E	F	G	H	I
J	K	L	M	N	O	P	Q	R
S	T	U	V	W	X	Y	Z	

Calculate the Heart's Desire Number

The first step is to calculate the heart's desire. Your heart's desire number describes what motivates you or your inner drives.

Adding the value of the vowels in each part of your birth name. For example, Jane Alexis Smith would be calculated 1 (a) + 5 (e) = 6 (Jane); 1 (a) + 5 (e) + 9 (i) = 15 (Alexis); 9

(i) (Smith)

Reduce each to a single digit by adding the individual digits of your first answer. For example, 6 (Jane); 1+ 5 = 6 (Alexis); 9 (Smith)

Next, add all the names together. 6 (Jane) + 6 (Alexis) + 9 (Smith) = 21

The final step is to reduce yet again to a single digit. 2 + 1 = 3

Calculate Your Personality Number

Here, you'll once again use your birth name, but calculate it using consonants of your name. Your personality number describes the image you project to the world.

1. Add the value of the consonants in each part of your birth name. For example,

Jane Alexis Smith would be calculated 1 (j) + 5 (n) = 6 (Jane); 3

(l) + 6 (x) + 1 (s) = 10 (Alexis); 1 (s) + 4 (m) + 2 (t) + 8 (h) = 15 (Smith).

2. Reduce each to a single visit. For example 6 (Jane); 1 +0 = 1 (Alexis); 1 + 5 =6 (Smith).

3. Add all the names together. For example 6 (Jane) + 1 (Alexis) + 6 (Smith) = 13

4. Reduce to a single digit. For example, 1 + 3 = 4.

Destiny Number

Your destiny number may also be called your expression number. It describes the opportunities and inner goals available to you. Use the full birth name to calculate it.

1. Add the value of all letters of your name at birth, creating a separate number for each name. For example: 1 (j) + 1 (a) + 5 (n) + 5 (e) = 12; 1 (a) + 3 (l) + 5 (e) + 6 (x) + 9 (i) + 1 (s)

= 25; 1 (s) + 4 (m) + 9 (i) + 2 (t) + 8 (h) = 24

2. Reduce each name to a single digit. For example, 1 + 2 = 3 (Jane); 2 + 5 = 7 (Alexis); 2+ 4 = 6 (Smith).

3. Now, add all numbers together. For example, 3 (Jane) + 7 (Alexis) + 6 (Smith) = 16

4. Reduce this final number. For example, 1 + 6 = 7.

Calculate Planes of Expression

If you've been adding correctly, you should now have three sets of numbers: the heart's desire, the personality number, and the destiny number. Now you're ready to calculate the planes of expression for these. These numbers are important because they can provide a detailed study ofthe manner in which an individual thinks, acts, and behaves. The planes can also help reveal inner conflicts, and they also play a significant role in love relationships. Use these rules for planes of expression to calculate the numbers that will provide information about mental, physical, emotional, and spiritual numerology specific to your birth name and your current name.

Calculate Your Life Path Number

Your life path number is derived from your birthday. It is an outline of your karmic imprint you bring into this lifetime inclusive of skills, challenges, and other things that may arise in your life.

Add your numbers for mm, dd, and yyyy separately. For example, for December 14, 1969, add 1

+ 3 = 3 (December); 1 + 4 = 5 (14); 1 + 9 + 6 + 9 = 25 (1969).

Reduce each number. For example, 3 (December); 5 (14); 2 + 5 = 7 (1969).

Now, add all numbers together. For example 3 (December) + 5 (14) + 7 (1969) = 15

Finally, reduce this to a single digit. For example, 1 + 5 = 6.

Calculate Your Attainment Number

In a numerology chart, attainment represents the spiritual consciousness under which many lives and rebirths have come into form. This number represents everything you have ever been (in a past life) and what you are striving for in this life. Numerologists look at the attainment number as the "design" of the soul's journey.

To calculate, add your destiny number to your life path number. For example, 7 (Jane's destiny number) + 6 (Jane's life path number) = 13

Reduce to a single digit. For example, 1 + 3 = 4

Master Numbers 11, 22, and 33

The only time you don't reduce a number to a single digit is if the result is a master number. There are three master numbers: 11, 22, and 33. In the final result of any calculation, leave this as it is and read the result for the master number, instead.

Junior, Senior, or Other Numbers in a Birth Name

If your name has a generational identifier, such as junior, senior, II, III, IV, etc., these aren't calculated into any of the numbers above, so you can simply drop them from the name.

How Name Changes Affect Your Numerology

If you've legally changed your name, you go by a nickname, or you have a maiden and married name or have obtained a hyphenated name, these can affect your numerology. You can also calculate with your new name to gain insights into how you may have changed in your life, but your basic karmic imprint comes from your given name at birth.

What the Numbers Mean

You can look up the meaning of each number on a number meaning numerology chart to glean information about each of the above aspects of your life.

Understanding Your Numbers

Calculating your numerology chart can help you gain a better understanding of some of the imprints, also called karmic overlays, you come into this lifetime with. As you gain a better understanding of these imprints, you can work to find solutions to navigate challenges that arise in your life based on the gifts you brought with you when you were born.

Easy Steps in Creating Your Own Numerology Report

1. First, let's start with your Birth Date. Write out your complete birth date that appears on your birth certificate on a piece of paper. This includes the month, day, and full year of your birth.

Numbers derived from your birth date are:

Your Life Path number

Your Birth Day number

Your Challenge numbers (first to fourth and main)

Your Pinnacle Cycles (first to fourth)

Your Period Cycles (first to third)

Your Current Personal Year Cycle

Your Expression of Destiny number o Your Heart's Desire

Your Personality

2. Translate the birth date into numbers. For example, March 26, 1953 becomes 3 for March; 2,6 for 26; and 1, 9, 5 and 3 for 1953.

3. Add each of the numbers all together. Using the above numbers, it would mean 3 + (2+6=) 8 + (1+9+5+3=18, add the 2 numbers further=1+8=) 9 = 3 +8 +9 = 20

4. Add the final two numbers (the sum) together. So, an equation that has an answer of 20 would result to 2 (2+0). This would be your life path number which is 2.

5. Look at the significance of your life path number at for your birth date. Each

number has different traits that are reflected by that number. You can see these traits from looking at numerology number meanings online at an astrology site or buy a book that discusses numerology.

Your Life Path number is at the heart of your being during this life. It describes what you arereally like and what is innate and natural for you. It is also the number of vibration in which

your soul has chosen to ground its life essence. Therefore, the energies present in your Life Path will feed on the opportunities, experiences, and lessons that you attract this life.

6. List down the traits below your calculated life path number.

7. Calculate other numerology numbers that can be derived from your birth dates like Expression, Heart's Desire, and Personality.

To find your Heart's Desire number:

Add the numerical value of the vowels of each of your names

Reduce them to single digits; add the single digits; and reduce them again to a single-digit number, which is your Heart's Desire number.

To find your Personality number:

Add the numerical value of the consonants of each of your names in the same manner as described earlier in Heart's Desire. Do not reduce the Master numbers 11 and 22 when calculating the Personality Number

The name Thomas has four consonants with the values of 2, 8, 4, and 1, which totals 15.

Fifteen reduces to 6.

The name Sam has two consonants with a combined numerical value of 5.

The name Lim has two consonants, which total 7. To find your Expression number:

Write out your full name, and place the appropriate numerical value beneath each letter

Add the numbers of your first name, and then reduce it to a single digit. Do the same for your middle and last names.

Now, add the three single-digit numbers, and reduce them to another single-digit number

to find your Expression number. If you encounter

Master number, 11, 22 or 33, do not reduce it to a single-digit number.

The number value of the letters in Thomas totals 22 (Master numbers are not reduced!).

The number value of the letters in Sam totals 6.

The number value of the letters in Lim totals 7.

His full name at birth totals 22+6+7=35.

Thomas Lim's Expression number is 3+5=8

8. Look at the meaning of these numbers. Like your life path, they have different meanings too.

9. List down all the traits that fall on these numbers on your report.

10. Finally, blend the major numerology numbers into one chart. You may add descriptive words that apply.

Numerology is an ancient method of analysing an individual and his/her life's directions, and gain guidance on the basis of numbers and their vibrations. To do that, one must construct a numerology chart. Does it include several numbers that are calculated on the basis of two sets of data? Name and date of birth. It is with the help of this data your numerology calculations are made.

Name or Expression Number

According to numerology, all the alphabets in the English language have been assigned a value. The name or expression number is the sum total of the entire name, reduced to a single digit. It describes how you interact with other people, how you express yourself, and where your talents lie.

Motivation Number

This is the sum total of the numerical values assigned to all the vowels (a, e, i, o, u) within the name, reduced to a single digit. This explains the motive behind the decisions that you take and the reasons behind how you act.

Inner-self Number

This is the sum total of the numerical values assigned to all the consonants within the name, reduced to a single digit. This describes what you are all about from within, how you look at yourself, and what your first impression may be like on other people.

Karmic Lesson Number

These are the lessons you are supposed to learn in this lifetime. These are numbers that do not exist in your name.

Subconscious Response Number

This describes how you will instinctively react in an emergency. To find this number, subtract the karmic lesson number from 9.

Hidden Tendencies

The number is present in your name in large amounts; i.e., the number appears several times in your name. This means that you are likely to go overboard with the qualities or tendencies that are described by that number.

Destiny Number

This is the sum total of your date of birth reduced to a single digit. This number shows you what is the ruling force in your life, and what you must do in order to achieve harmony in your life.

Birth Number

This is the sum total of your day of birth, reduced to a single digit. This number shows you what influences are prevalent in your life.

Life Cycles

This is the calculation of the inherent cycles of one's life. According to numerology, there are only 3 life cycles.

• First Cycle - This is the sum of your month of birth, reduced to a single digit. This cycle lasts from the time of your birth till you attain maturity. To find out when this cycle ends, subtract your Destiny Number from 36 and then add 1 to get the number.

• Second Cycle - This is the sum of your day of birth, reduced to a single digit. This cycle lasts for 27 years after the first cycle has ended.

• Third Cycle - This is the sum total of your birth year, reduced to a single digit. This cycle begins once the second cycle has ended, and lasts till you die.

Turning Points

This describes the events that may occur during a given Life Cycle. There is a grand total of 4 Turning points.

• First Turning Point - This is the sum total of the day and month of birth, reduced to a single digit. It lasts during the time of your First Cycle.

• Second Turning Point - This is the sum total of the day and year of birth, reduced to a single digit. It begins once the First Turning Point ends, and lasts for 9 years.

• Third Turning Point - This is the sum total of the First and Second Turning Points, reduced to a single digit. It begins once the Second Turning Point ends, and lasts for 9 years.

• Fourth Turning Point - This is the sum total of the month and year of birth, reduced to a single digit. It starts once the Third Turning Point ends, and lasts till you die.

Challenges

These describe your weaknesses and the hurdles that you will face in life. There are 3 challenges (2 minor and 1 major) in life.

• First Minor Challenge - Take the day of birth and month of birth, and reduce it to a single digit each. Then subtract the smaller number from the bigger number.

• Second Minor Challenge - Take your day and year of birth, and reduce it to a single digit each. Then subtract the smaller number from the bigger number.

• Major Challenge - Take both the minor challenge numbers and subtract the smaller number from the bigger number.

Example

Now let us look at an example, so that the entire process is clarified even better:

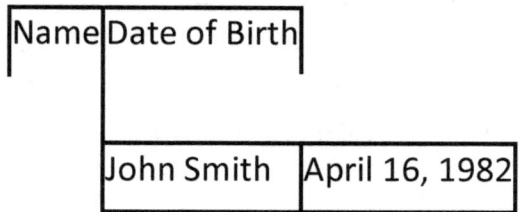

Name	Date of Birth
John Smith	April 16, 1982

Name or Expression Number John = 1 + 6 + 8 + 5

Smith = 1 + 4 + 9 + 2 + 8

This gives us 44 = 4 + 4 = 8 Name or Expression Number = 8

Motivation Number

The vowels present in the entire name are: 'o' and 'i', so, 6 + 9 = 15 and 1 − 5 = 6 Motivation Number = 6

Chapter 2: Independence And The Entrepreneur Of Many Colors

The Sun rules 1. The Sun is the center of our solar system and, with the Moon, is the source of all life-giving energies on our planet. The Sun influences the number 1, and a strong Leo or fire influence may be present in the astrological chart of a 1 Birthday. This Birthday number will greatly empower any air (Gemini, Libra, and Aquarius) or water (Cancer, Scorpio, and Pisces) sun sign.Even when working for someone else, 1 Birthdays are independent to the hilt. Personal autonomy, physical freedom and mobility are of the utmost importance. A 1's idea of freedom is more outward than inward. This is why they do best working for themselves or having a job in which they have little or no supervision. They make good leaders, but are not always happy as supervisors or managers. In spite of the leadership abilities that go with a 1

Birthday, 1s don't always make the best leaders. The number 1 in any number cycle always signifies something to do with independence or the lack of it, depending on the placement of the 1. A 1 Birthday doesn't want to control anything more than his own world. He does well as an initiator or instigator. Martin Luther, who was at the forefront of the first successful break from the Catholic Church, was a prime example of a 1 Birthday: an independent, intelligent leader, initiator and instigator.

A 1 Birthday's loneliness comes not from being out of place, but from being out in front. 1 truly is very lonely for many of you born on a 1 day. 1 Birthdays are difficult to pin down. Just when you think you have them where you want them, they go in a different direction. They are reliable, but they need to go their own way. People born on the 1st and the 19th are among the most intrinsically aggressive individuals you will meet.

These people need to lead in a close relationship, especially people born on the 1st and the 19th. They sometimes come across as controlling because that's how they treat their lives and personal space and anyone who enters that space or life feels the control. A 1 Birthday isn't the type who wants to control the world, just their own space. They are so concerned with preserving their personal freedom. Women in this Birthday group think like men and sometimes take the masculine role in a relationship. A 1 woman sometimes thinks more like a man than many men she meets. A mature 1 woman is among the most assertive of any woman. A strong 1 Birthday woman might marry because of social conditioning or personal need, yet her needs in a man and close relationship are very exacting, so she should choose carefully. If she forces herself to settle for less than what she wants. She, more so than most females of other number make ups, will be frustrated and feel unfulfilled if having to settle for less. However, she would remain very devoted to any man she marries. A 1 man wants to feel as unrestrained as possible while having the comfort and security of home life. A 1 Birthday man or woman is the best candidate to remain single, if he chooses, because he doesn't need another to feel complete. At worst, a 1 Birthday can be aloof, stubborn and self-centered.

Any façade number, except the 2, is conducive toward the 1 Birthday's independent nature. People born on the 1st can turn flashes of intuition into practical, working, even money-making ideas. People born on the 19th are among the most aggressive (because of the 9 influence), and 10th natives are the most dreamy and intuitive (because of the Zero influence). They might not have as much get up and go as the other 1 Birthdays, but they have more moments of insight and spiritual connection that other 1 Birthdays are too busy to notice.

Two Number 1 Birthdays would be quite a fire match in any sort of relationship, but in love, they might have problems jousting for rule of the castle. Because of the strong need to feel unencumbered, a 1 Birthday of either sex would do best having few or no children.

Chapter 3: Success Numbers And Practice

The universe of number is infinite. Therefore, many other calculations can be made to balance and make good use of your numerology. The three calculations used above are excellent for getting insight into your personal natural makeup, but other numbers hold a more general influence over everyday life. These numbers can vary from culture to culture and change over time, but let's discuss some other ways to calculate for specific reasons and other notable numbers and their personalities.

With these numbers, as well as the main three above, you can work with them to achieve your desires and time your plans to be on favorable days. Some dedicated numerologists have mastered the art of forecasting, being able to anticipate major life events and even manipulate them. These practices go hand in hand with astrology, but more on that later.

Numbers for prosperity

Many people find their way to numerology in search of assistance with monetary gain. Everyone could use a little more money in their pocket and numerology can help. Once you've learned your personal numerology choose a favorable line of work that suits your natural make-up. Also planning certain events, such as job interviews or job-hunting days, on favorable days will assist you in gaining consistent income.

It is good to keep in mind there is no 'get rich quick' scheme to be done with numerology. While working with these numbers will increase the probability of you receiving your desired outcome, if the odds are against you in a great way you may not see immediate results. The lottery is a good example. If you have a 1 in 1,000,000 chance to win and your work with numerology lessens that to 1 in 900,000 chance it still has been successful numerological work, but you would never know and the chances are still stacked against you. Choose wisely how you spend your time and focus on finding ways to generate income since a nice job is more likely that 1 million dollars falling into your lap. Be creative and specific in your workings.

1 1 is a great number to work with if you are seeking prosperity. This number is thought to be key in achieving success, consider the ideas of being number one in a ranking system or being the first to do something. Choosing 1, 10, 19 or 28 as days to start new jobs or searching for jobs is recommended.

The number 1 may also be used to start new ventures or transition into a better position in the job you already have. Start new projects on these dates and anticipate these dates as days of change and growth.

Working with the sun as a symbolic version of 1 is helpful as well. Sundays that are 1, 10, 19 or 28 dates are especially potent for 1 energy. Offerings can be left to the sun in the form of water, incense and of course, money. This work is especially potent and should be handled with respect and humility.

2 The number two is thought to be unfavorable for financial gain. The 2 energy often delays things, often having to attempt things twice to succeed. While the numbers 11 and 22 are known for abundance, this could be elusive for money. It is recommended that job searching and asking for raises should not be done on day 2, 11, 20 and 29.

3 The number 3 can be tricky to work with for prosperity purposes. Although known for acquiring wealth, it is often emotional or loving wealth, rather than money. If 3 is heavy in your numerology, it will require intense focus to gain and maintain monetary wealth. Spontaneous spending should be avoided.

4 If you have trouble keeping jobs, 4 may be able to help, but this number requires discipline and hard work. If you work with your hands, 4 can help you maintain your job and acquire raises. Investing time and hard work goes well with the dates 4, 8, 13, 22, 31.

5 The number five works well with financial situations, a dedicated career benefits from the 5 energy, but savings and investments are a must if you have heavy 5 energy in your personal numerology. Days 5, 14 and 23 are excellent days to seek investment opportunities and open bank accounts.

6 The number 6 works well for abundant prosperity; this influence is very prominent later in life. Working with six to prepare for retirement or save money for big adventures is recommended. Days 6, 15 and 24 are great days to take care of debts and plan future finances.

7 The number 7 can go either way with financial situations. Financial challenges and significant financial gains are common with heavy 7 influence. This is risky to work with for prosperity so isn't generally recommended unless it places well with other numerological or astrological factors.

8 The number 8 is great for prosperity; this number is so organized and driven towards financial gain that it is almost unavoidable if you want to be materially wealthy. Logical and calm days 8, 17 and 26 are great for hard working days and finishing projects. 8 energy is necessary to complete tasks in a timely manner so pairs well with the 2 energy, 8+2=10, 1+0=1, and so you also get the 1 energy from these workings.

8 may cause some troubles along the way in the form of deadlines and disrupted timelines. Saturn is the planetary ruler of 8 and dictates time and logic. Working with Saturn can be risky so approach at your own risk with offerings or ritual workings.

9 The number 9 energy attracts prosperity constantly, but the influence also creates a lack of material desire. This can be good for acquiring small sums of money quickly but will be spent immediately. The unique features of 9 will allow you to gain money, but it will have to be with the intention of using the money for selfless reasons, such as charitable works and humanitarian change.

Numbers for love

For relationships and love numerology we will be predominantly be using life path numbers, but these numbers can be worked with on their own as well to find compatibility and balanced relationships, platonic or romantic.

Some systems of numerology find that if two people share a life path number that they are compatible as having much in common, but may not find growth within the relationship. Numbers that are opposites may have differing viewpoints, but the opposite opinions offer room for growth and stimulating conversation.

While many numbers can be compatible with a wide array of different number combinations, we will discuss the attributes of each life path number as a lover and friend below.

1 In relationships, this number loves to be in charge. Being straightforward and self-reliant is key to this number's compatibility. The need to be in control can lead to self-conscious behavior if they feel like things are out of their control. Creative activities and exercises are a must and consistency are needed.

2 In relationships, the number two really enjoys being a couple. Sharing responsibilities and living as much of their lives as possible with their companions is an ultimate goal. As a romantic partner, this number is sensitive but also empathetic in a great way. Constant affection and teamwork are key.

3 In relationships, life path number 3 natives may seem casual and not invested, but deep down they're very kind and caring. Socializing and hosting gatherings is one way that this number shows its affection. As a romantic partner, the outer shell may need to be cracked to get their reciprocated affection.

4 In relationships, this number is devoted and strong. Being able to uplift their companions, the life path 4 natives are nurturing and attentive. Material gain and emotional balance are key to this number's personal life. Spontaneity and adventures are great since this number is so reliable and enjoyable to be around.

5 Communication is key for relations with life path 5 natives. Their conversation is witty and original and they expect the same from their partners. Physical appearances need to be distinct and socializing is needed to please this number's desire to stimulate all the senses. Going out to eat or to concerts is a great way to please the number 5

6 The number 6 has long been associated with beauty and sex. Venus is the ruling planet for this number and it shows. As a companion this number loves to be responsible for its family and friends, cleaning, cooking and all around caring for the day to day tasks needed to keep a home. These partners are quick to empathize and love fixing a bad day or adverse scenario.

7 For relationships, life path 7 is mysterious and powerful. Intellectual or spiritual conversation is very important, as well as adventures to meaningful places, like ruins or mountains. With magical tendencies, these companions may seek universal truths and expect your assistance, be prepared for intense, out of this world energy.

8 As we learned in the prosperity section, 8 is a great number for logic and money. These things come through in relationships as well. Balance and strength give this number a very attractive quality for those seeking foundation and security.

Material goals and adventures abound as you spend time with these natives, they typically love to brag about their lovers and friends.

9 This number has an 'old soul' mentality when it comes to relationships. Deep, insightful conversations and mental clarity is key to pleasing the number 9. Having a compassionate attitude toward humanity is also very important; charitable work and volunteering is a huge part of this number's life. Showing immense love for their partners and the whole world, this unique number is unforgettable as a companion.

Motivational numbers

These numbers are relatively new in the numerology sphere. It is calculated by finding the value of only the vowels in your full name and then reducing that number to a single digit if it isn't already one. This number reveals hidden emotions and desires, thus motivating one to aspire toward these desires. Fears may be revealed or even other obstacles that may be secretly hindering you from achieving what you want. Contemplation on these numbers is very therapeutic for confidence and mental clarity.

Let's take a look at the individual numbers and what they may be hiding about your true self. This revealing calculation may be eye-opening too many, but keep in mind that you may have unhealthy desires and well as balanced ones. Be aware of which is which.

1 Motivational number 1 reveals your desire to be the center of attention. You wish to be a leader and feel that you have the best answers. You are content as long as you are in control of any given situation. You secretly wish you could work alone since you have the best ideas. A desire to be the first to accomplish something or be number one on a competitive list is common. This can manifest into narcissism and lack of empathy if left unchecked.

2 Motivational number two reveals to you that you desperately need peace in your day to day life. The less the change and drama, the better. The basic necessities and a small circle of loved ones are all it takes to motivate you. You wish to have a significant other that can be the hub of your life. Harmony and routine are ideal, and adventure is not favored.

3 The motivational number 3 desires fame and glamour, with emphasis on entertaining others. Your popularity is important to you and you gauge your success on how well-liked you are. Home décor and appearances need to be fashionable and contemporary. The desire for constant attention and interaction with others is constant, as well as wanting to spread creative ideas and share yourself with others.

4 Deep down, the motivational number 4 wants everything to be structured and logical. If each detail of your life could be meticulously planned, then you would do it. Material structure and organization are desired at all times. You feel it is your responsibility to build a balanced home and environment. Practicality is a motivating force that is unavoidable.

5 The motivational number five desperately needs freedom and change. Having the freedom you want will allow you to cater to other needs such as adventure and experiences that are not mundane. Stimulation of the five senses is required constantly and may become obsessive. Making new friends and lovers is a common desire as well

6 As a motivational number, 6 reveals your desire to create a harmonious life. You value fairness and can't stand injustice. You wish to teach others and help as many people as possible if you can't contribute in helpful ways, then you are unfulfilled. You have a fiery need to create and be expressive throughout day to day life.

7 Motivational number 7 imparts an intense desire to be alone. Quiet meditation and studying are ideal ways to spend your free time; without this much needed alone time, you may be restless and scatterbrained. Privacy is needed to achieve these goals, and deep down you may want to be alone the majority of the time. Communication through intelligible conversation is necessary. Retreats into nature for indefinite amount of time are fitting

8 Motivational number 8 reveals a hungry need for material gain and power. This attitude can easily become uncontrollable; you may feel like you would do anything to achieve authority or riches. You want to own all the latest technology, buy nice cars and overall really show off your wealth. You wish to tell others what to do, boasting your material success to prove that your way is best.

9 You have an undying desire to broaden your spiritual capabilities and learn about the true nature of reality. You desperately want others to join you on your spiritual quests and humanitarian endeavors. Your emotions get the best of you since you feel so strongly toward the entire universe; this can be tough to balance at times. Practicality alludes you as you think with your emotions, chasing idealistic goals rather than material ones.

Personal growth numbers

11 and 22

These numbers hold a distinct energy that we need to discuss briefly. These numbers are considered 'master numbers.' This is in reference to the fact that these numbers are more adept at spiritual conquest. Added awareness and powers of perception are endowed with the influence of these numbers. Many who have these numbers as life path numbers often feel strange or have run-ins with the paranormal. This may lead one to think they have a problem but, in fact, they are more conscious of other worlds and various other intelligence.

If these added powers of the spiritual nature are ignored, there may be consequences that cannot be reversed.

This is a huge responsibility that is owed to the individual and humanity as a whole. Some use these powers for evil purposes to gain selfish desires; this should be avoided as well. With added pressure to be a cosmic hero to humanity, these numbers as life path numbers should be handled with care. It is recommended to seek out a spiritual teacher if these numbers are heavy in your numerology.

Chapter 4: Understanding The Power Of The Symbols

You have been told earlier that the symbols hold a great importance in your life and when you are trying to understand your future or are even trying to read the future for someone else.

Power of a Name

Names create an impression that is instantaneous. You may love your name and will also find people all around you who love their name too. There are some people who may be uncomfortable with wanting to change their names while there are others who may want to change their names. Different names always sound very different and always leaving you with a different feeling that would feel like energy. When you look at your newborn baby, you may call her or him by a name. You will find that your child will look up at you and smile when you use that name.

This is because of the fact that the baby loves the name you have given it. This is the same with dogs too! You may find it difficult to believe that this can actually happen but it does happen. You can try it with your dog at home or you could also go to a kennel and call a pup by a name and see if he turns to you.

You will realize over the course of the book that your names are not accidental and do have their own vibrations and also help you fulfill your mission to learn more about yourself. You will find that the names of people will always have a reason behind it. There are some names that are so common that you will find a phone book filled with these names. There are some people who have formed groups because they have the same name and also have the same occupation and tend to think the same way at all times.

There are experts who say that people with common names tend to show contempt on another person with the same name. Over the centuries, people all over the world would approach and address each other with the titles of Mister, Misses or Miss which helped them all get along with one another since that helped them treat each other with a sense of respect. These days, people have started to call each other by name that makes these people very personal to them.

There are times when people have associated names with the things invented by them, for instance they have said Salk vaccine or Disneyland which fit their inventions in the perfect sense. Would you prefer it if these names were interchanged? What if Disneyland went by the name of Salkland? Or what if an opera were to play at Disneyland instead of playing at the Sydney Opera House? You would have seen that in the advertising world, the names of people are what make money. There are numerous corporations that have started to pay a large sum of money to identify the right name for a product. The names of different cities are also important since that name could affect a whole community. It is a fact that a great name is greater than having an ointment in hand.

Power of a Word

You may have heard the phrase, 'Here are the temples of his word'. These words are living entities. These are given life when they are said by a man and always live in the fourth dimension since they start residing in the crossover. You will find that the spiritual structures finally start making sense when you have understood the power of words. The word that is spoken has more power since it always brings forth a thought which would always start at the manifestation of that very thought. This is because of the fact that what you say always comes out from the heart. This states that you will always say what appeals to you most and what lies in your consciousness. You will always reveal this level of consciousness through the words that you speak.

In the Kabbalah it has been said that the name of God is always found with the vowel sounds in it since these sounds form the vibrations of life. You could try an experiment and read this entire paragraph without using the sound of the vowels. You will find that the sound produced makes no sense without the vowels and is called the animated spirit of the world. Every sound can be measured by the way it has been spoken and the vibration that has been created on being pronounced. You can obtain the picture of the vibration that is created by using a device called the eidophone. This is an instrument that looks like a drum and has a rubber material on its top. There is a mouthpiece that extends from it which is used to speak the sound. The crystalline mixture that is found on the top of the instrument forms different pictures based on the sounds that have been produced. For instance, when a person says the word butterfly, the crystals create a shape of a beautiful butterfly and when you say dog, the crystals take the shape of a dog. These lovely words form the loveliest pictures. There are harsh words that produce absolutely no image. They are haphazard and may even seem ugly when looked at closely. The invisible meaning of the words always takes a form when you say the word aloud. This is why the words you say or speak are the most important! It is because of this that it is said that a wise man may be a fool if he has the lips of a fool!

Power of thought

You had read earlier that a spoken word is what manifests a thought in the universe that is the start of the process. This is a subject that has been discussed for years. There are people who are still trying to analyze if the forms that exist have a scientific basis for them! There are people who are trying to work towards developing a form for thought through numerous experiments.

The first step to this was to relax their minds and also bring their brains into the state of the alpha to ensure that the brain waves can be the masters of thought. He would then start describing a dragon and while he did that the students in the class would have to picture ever word of the description. Only when their thoughts were unified would a mist begin to form. This mist would take the shape of a dragon and always held the form till the students began to lose the power to concentrate. This helped them conclude that the thoughts that a person has are always in a state of motion and if people start to think collectively, they would become extremely powerful! This is when you may start to wonder about how you can start sensing certain thought forms when you are in a place where there are people who are all thinking the very same thing – for instance the shopping mall or even a bar. There is definitely a certain mood that is connected with each place. These moods and the thought forms have all been developed by the atmosphere of the location.

There are a lot of people around the world who may be psychic but would have never been able to identify that they were that. These people tend to pick up on thought forms with ease. When you have understood these forms you will start to realize that these forms are not supernatural at all! Your words will always leave a thought that would continue to exist. This is because of the fact that the words you speak produce a thought that would always be a part of your energy that has its very own vibration. When a vibration of this magnitude is sent out by a tuning fork, you will find that the vibrations are projected on objects of the same frequency and it is because of this that the other object begins to vibrate too! But, objects of a different frequency will always remain unfazed or untouched by these vibrations.

Your whole body is always in action when it comes to your thoughts. All your muscles and your larynx move which may or not may be detectable. There are a few scientists who have discovered that your chest movements are directly related to your thoughts and have also succeeded in recording the patterns of those thoughts graphically. Every thought that you have always has a set wavelength.

It was in the year 1945 that a professor and doctor, Sir Alexander Cannon, had learned to compare different thoughts through a mathematical interpretation of the graphs. These graphs also helped in showing the effect that different types of music had on different people. These graphs also show greater things: they say that the thoughts of one person could always influence another through the mental atmosphere that surrounds these thoughts. You will be able to detect these thoughts through respiration. You will always be able to control your thoughts by proper breathing. You will be told how this can be done in the latter part of the book. This is good to know since you will be able to maintain a balance in your mind and it is also beneficial for your body. You have to use certain mantras too which help in meditation. It is always good to either say the mantras aloud or to even whisper them. But, the best way to ensure that you gain power is by repeating the mantra in your thoughts. This is never surprising since you can hear your inner voice only when you are quiet. You will be able to cure diseases by repeating thoughts of contentment. When you start worrying too much and fill your mind with inharmonious thoughts, you are filing yourself up with negativity, which would create numerous diseases. This is because of the fact that your immune system always releases adrenaline when it believes you are in danger. This happens when you start worrying too much and place yourself under immense stress. At the very same time, your heart begins to beat faster which will release acid into your stomach. Your body can never explain the difference between actual danger and the idea or a thought of danger. When your mind is the only thing worried, you will find that your body begins to prepare itself anyway! If there are too many hormones produced in your body, you will be causing yourself immense physical problems that would lead to the deterioration of your body. It is always good to gain a control over your thoughts and emotions to maintain great health. People may look the same on the outside but it is their chemical composition which helps you either like them or dislike them since it is these compositions which would help you find someone who has the same level of consciousness as you!

It is the consciousness that exists within people that helps in setting up their personal rates of vibrations. People of the same mind are always in tune with each other in reality. Every human being is like a tuning fork and you will find that a person who has a completely different rate of vibration would never seem attractive to you. Your own vibration is recorded in your auric field. A person who is more knowledgeable always has a vibration with a shorter wavelength and a higher frequency. It is this level of vibration that manifests itself in your voice. It is always the tone of your voice that decides the level of spiritual development. You will find that the level of vibrations is also available when you are reading. When you are reading while comprehending, you will see the printed word and will also see the form of the word in your mind's eye. This goes to say that you are visualizing and reading the word at the very same time.

Every person has his or her own ability to comprehend or understand anything in the world. You will find that people will obtain different meaning from the very same verse or paragraph that has been read by them. The extent to your knowledge is always dependent on your expectations from life and your thoughts. You always draw opinion from a personal safe house where you have saved all your beliefs, reactions and actions. These have the strongest influence on your vision since they have an effect on the optic nerve that always stores them in your very own picture gallery in your mind. Whatever you see or hear is always stored in your brain and it is these thoughts that appear in your dreams when you are asleep. These thoughts and images take colorful forms and appear in your dreams.

Chapter 5: The Purpose Of Numbers

Success in life is by a big percentage down to the feat you apply in your day to day activities aimed at achieving your goals. However, hard work is not the sole determinant here. The role of numbers, if well understood and well used cannot be over looked. Yes, millions of people are successes out there without using numbers and numerology, because they don't find them necessary, or, they don't even know numerology exists in the first place. But that is no reason enough to make you conclude that numbers don't apply with everyone. First of all, it's true these guys are successes – and without numerology. But how do we know they reached their full potential? The point here is; success is immeasurable and these people – maybe – could be more prosperous if they included numbers in their effort.

Below are a few areas where numerology can be used to influence the circumstances and events that will be part and parcel of your future.

Baby Naming

According to numerology, some of the events and circumstances we have encountered throughout our lives are an effect of numbers that are connected with the names we bear. Some names are connected to numbers that are considered generally lucky or embodying prosperous futures, while some carry numbers that predict futures of hardships and struggle.

Any name, though, if studied and interpreted early enough, can still be the spur of a good life because numerology is not only about what your numbers represent but also how you can use them to change you fate to a more desirable one.

Off course we all imagine the kind of futures we want for our dear little ones, and we know that certain names bearing certain numbers are considered "luckier" than others. But, can we use this knowledge to guarantee our children good lives. No off course not – and I repeat, no. Why? Because naming is not the sole determinant of the kind of events and circumstances that have an influence of one's life. The effect of naming according to numerologists, though, cannot be overlooked, but it doesn't mean that you go asking for numerologists on which name to give your newborn.

Still on baby naming, another concept that frequently crops up is reincarnation. Whether you believe in it or not doesn't matter much, but if you do, the idea put forward is simple. Your newborn is arriving to continue the journey of learning things only learnable on this plane. You, as the mother, have already spent enough time with this little blessing. You may have subliminally grasped some clues on the things this reincarnated tot would want to have for a handle. Mom should thus take the lead in figuring it out, with a little help from dad. But generally, I think, in this process, she should be the ultimate arbiter.

Name Changing

One of the most frequently asked questions over the years has had something to do with name changes. The effect on success and destiny brought about by name changes. Most numerology guides spend a lot of their ink trying to figure out the "destiny number" or expression that is exclusively based on the official birth name. The expression is right at the top alongside date of birth as the most significant factors in today's numerology. The official expression or destiny number explains the development, direction of growth and what you should achieve. This name together with the number connected to it stays with you during your entire life. But, how about the name we are recognized with in our daily business, our professional and public lives, in our marriages and with our friends?

Professional names in your writing, music or acting career, nicknames you are given in some life stages or even during your whole life, your married name, and even a short version of your full name, are among the name changes you may go through in your life time. Almost each and every one of us has had a series of names that has passed into and out of usage throughout our lives. To assess your changed name, look at the name you commonly go by and how you could you meet people and get introduced to them.

Each and every name we are identified by at some points in our lives has a specific meaning. If you have the power to influence the name you receive, just choose one connected to the number or numbers that bear the traits you admire. You should however avoid using names that overemphasize the number you choose because, this way, negative traits associated with the number tend to surface as well.

Numbers and Career

Attending school for a course you are not vocationally connected to can have an effect on your future life for the worse. Numerology can help you choose a career. Experts reveal that more than 80% of estimates based on numerology are accurate.

Using formulas that are discussed later in this book, you can find out the numbers connected to career names you are interested in and see if they match. Simply, if your Life Path number is five, try looking for a career that has the same number or any other number whose traits are similar to that five.

Numbers and Relationships

Before you get to make the ultimate decision on the person you want to spend the rest of your life with, a little help from numbers is worthwhile. Some relationships appear perfect from the beginning but that sometimes is never the case when marriage sets in. A marriage followed immediately by divorce or constant quarrels with the person who should be your main source of joy should qualify as the worst love story ever. So how do you ensure the relationship you are in will work?

Here also, your Life Path numbers come into play.

First, you need to know your Life Path number and that of your partner. A matching number is good if you are fine with a partner you share traits with. But, most people prefer complementary traits to matching ones because stronger relationships are built by partners who have good but varying rather than similar qualities. At least you have something to learn from your partner in such a relationship.

Chapter 6: Intro To Numerology

Numerology is one of the easiest of the occult arts to understand and implement in your life, and it actually is one that you can get started with easily. This chapter will talk about what you need to do in order to fully understand what you're seeing when you look at the numbers that are presented to you.

What you need to get started with this is the birth date, and the name of the person that you're trying to look at and predict the secrets of. That's all you need to get started.

Now, there are eleven numbers that are used when it comes to constructing numerology charts. The numbers are 1, 2, 3, 4, 5, 6, 7, 8, 9, 11, and 22. If you see larger numbers, these are created from adding the numbers in the complete birth date, or form the values are given to each name, and they are also reduced by adding each of the digits together until you have a sum of one of the core numbers. Only adding the parts of the larger number together is done, until you have either a single digit, or a master number. However, each of these numbers does show a different characteristic or an expression.

For example, let's say that you have a name that comes out to the number 121. Obviously that's not one of those basic numbers, but if you add the 1, 2, and the 1 together, you get 4, which is one of the basic numbers. It's a way to really help you see what you're getting into, and it can help you with predicting the future of this chart.

The only exception to the rule of having a single digit is a master number, which is 11 and 22. These are well can be also seen as an intensified version of the single digit they replace, which would be 2 and 4. These numbers will suggest in this case a potential for a high degree of learning, achievement, and success in a stressful environment. In most of these people, the master numbers will operate as a more tangible and practical tool, and they are essentially the same as the single-digit parallel it has.

Now, what you first want to do is to take the date of birth. This is seen normally as mm/dd/yyyy and can determine the life path number and other factors. The concept of a life path number will be discussed later on.

You also will be converting the full birth name into the number, and as you continue you will see that the letters and numbers are always one in the same. To really see what you're getting from this, you need to look at the chart below and determine the numbers.

123456789

ABCDEFGHI

JKLMNOPQR

STUVWXYZ

As you can see, these numbers will have a value, so you take all of those and add them up over time. Now, you will see on your birth certificate the full birth name that you have. That's the name you want to use, often complete with a middle name. However, let's say that you have a nickname, or a name change, or even some marriage names that you have. Well, those aren't counted in this, and you use your original name without anything changed with it. You must use that, because it will help to fully allow one to recognize the importance of the name given to you and the life path that you're about to take.

Now that you know a bit about what numerology is and a brief introduction, it's time to delve into what everything means, and you will soon see just what you're capable of, and what each of the numbers in each of these different elements mean for you.

Chapter 7: The Meaning Of Master Numbers

Here are the Master numbers that you need to use in numerology in order to understand yourself:

One

Number one is outright masculine. Its symbol is the sun from where the world derives natural energy. Not surprisingly then, people whose Master number is one have lots of energy. They also exude confidence and firmness in decision making. Above all, number ones are an optimistic lot who do not fear to pursue their great ambitions.

However, the flip side of being a number one is that you may come across as bossy, pushy or overbearing. And that is because you tend to look forward decisively, oblivious of other people around you. Whereas you have good intentions in taking the lead, some of the people moving with you may feel ignored or underrated.

Two

Number Two carries femininity. Its symbol is the moon. People who fall under this category tend to be diplomatic and peace seekers. They are amongst the kindest people you could find, who like to see truth and justice prevail.

What you may not like about number twos is their vulnerability. They often come across as weak and sometimes cowardly.

Three

Three bears traits of masculinity. It is a number whose symbol is Mercury. It also happens to be representative of the divine triangle – call it God, His son as well as the Holy Spirit. Not surprisingly, people with three as their Master number are exemplary mediators. They are also great communicators who love harmony. You will also find them very sociable and very active.

Whereas communication is a good thing and mediation too, people who fall under this category often come across as not sincere; kind of, superficial.

Four

Four is feminine. Its symbol happens to be Saturn. It is also associated with the four main seasons of the year — summer, autumn, spring and winter. Still, you could equate it to a cube's four sides. And with that evenness, people under this number are stable and tend to do be dedicated workers. Often, though, they are too dedicated for comfort — failing to take necessary breaks and leisure time.

Five

This is a masculine number whose symbol is the star. Mars also symbolizes this number that is also depicted by your four limbs together with your head. People under this number are free spirits. They face challenges head on and enjoy adventure.

However, though their quick thinking and problem solving mindset helps them handle challenges better than most people, sometimes they take that boldness too far, making them seem a bit reckless. You also cannot always predict their mood as they happen to be quick tempered.

Six

Six is a feminine number whose symbol is Venus. People under this number are all motherly. They exude that warmth of a mother; tend to give a lot and nurture; and also appear to have the motherly instincts. They are very supportive and will make you feel secure and protected.

Even then, not everyone takes their good intentions kindly. Number sixes sometimes come across as too meddling and people do not like it when you nose around their affairs.

Seven

Number seven is masculine and its symbol is Neptune. People with seven as their

Master number happen to be highly intuitive. They often seem to let themselves search introspectively in a kind of spiritual manner. They are fine remaining alone for long durations and do not even put much effort into acquisition of property.

The intellect of number sevens cannot, however, be underrated. From this category you often find people with psychic abilities.

Despite the fact that the traits already mentioned are admirable, number sevens are bad for company. They seem cold to other people because of that tendency of losing themselves into inward thinking.

Eight

Eight is feminine and its symbol is Pluto. People with this Master number are hard workers who do all they can to become successful and wealthy.

However, in their single mindedness to find success, the eights become pushy and insensitive to the feelings of other people.

Nine

Nine is masculine and its symbol happens to be Jupiter. Number nine are highly intellectual people who are also high in energy. They are passionate and amiable; generous and compassionate; bearing lots of wisdom; and they also have tendencies of an artistic nature and originality. They tend to look at things from a global perspective.

However, these great characteristics are sometimes neutralized by the number nine fears of oncoming challenges. Also in their passion to accomplish things, they sometimes come across as somewhat insensitive to the feelings of other people. Besides, it is not always a good thing that they tend to forget the successes they have had fast while looking into the future.

Eleven

This is one Master number with masculinity as well as femininity. Its symbol is a combination of Jupiter and

Saturn. And you can appreciate the situation when you consider that this two digit number has the qualities of Number One as well as those of their sum, which is Number Two. And since one is masculine and two is feminine, number 11 carries the attributes from both. This gives number eleven people a likeable balance.

They are, however, a highly intuitive lot that does not like anything close to limitations and monotony. You will usually find them in the clergy and fields of communication like broadcasting.

Twenty-two

Number twenty-two is feminine. They are symbolized by a combination of Saturn and Pluto. It also carries the qualities of both the two of its individual digits, as well as the qualities of its sum, four. Under this number you get great planners who do well in leadership.

Sometimes, however, they take on too much in terms of work and responsibility.

Chapter 8: Master Numbers

IN THE PREVIOUS Section, you learned about the Cycles of Numerology and how the five Core numbers are calculated. Here you will discover exactly how the results of your personal readings will impact your life.

The process of calculating Master numbers is to add all the numbers of your birth date and birth name. Should the sum total be an 11, 22, or 33, you have what is referred to as a Master number. You don't have to reduce it to a single digit, but it will take on some of the traits of the single digit.

Example #1: 10/5/1960

1+0+5+1+9+6+0=22

This person has a 22 Master number Life Path.

Example #2: 9/11/1971

9+1+1=11
9+1+1+1+9+7+1=29/11

This person has a Master number 11 birth day as well as an 11 life path. Then you add the 1+1=2 and the 11 Master will take on the traits of a 2.

Note: when numbers repeat they become stronger. The above example has the Master number 11 in the Life Path and Birth Day. Lots of responsibility here to honor their gift; if they don't their life will be one of craziness.

Why? Because 1+1=2. 2 is ruled by the moon, and the moon is the Luna and you can become a Luna-TIC.

Numbers 1-9 Explained

THIS BOOK CERTAINLY is not intended to take the place of a full reading with an experienced numerologist. It is designed to provide you basic information so you can follow your intuition to learn more about who you are and work with the timing. It's all about timing...

YOU ARE MEANT to be a leader. You are very independent. You are an idea person, a pioneer, and a creator. You have drive and determination. You are full of energy and enjoy nature as well. Many law enforcement, military, self-employed, and craftsmen are born under a Life Path 1.

You resist anything or anyone that stands in your way of achieving your goal. You are driven. Once you make up your mind, there is no stopping you. You must learn to ask for help. You can't do it alone; you just think you can. You have the ability to manifest easily. It's your determination that gives you the ability to overcome challenges or obstacles. You set high standards for yourself and you enjoy surrounding yourself with like-minded people. You have no patience when you are around people who don't get you. This is why you assume the responsibility to be the protector and provider for your loved ones, because you feel no one can take on the task better than you. You command respect and attention and become quite cranky when things don't go your way.

You seek the forefront and the limelight. You can be a bit unusual. Your approach to problems is unique and you have the courage to think outside the box. You are an innovator. Your status and appearance of success and self-satisfaction are important to you as this keeps you motivated on your quest to success and growth. "Think it, act it, 'til you make it;" that's you. You enjoy the finer things in life and have no problem working to attain your desires.

On the negative side, watch out for selfishness, conceit, and being overly concerned with your appearance. You must be careful not to become aggressive and nasty in your behavior. If these qualities are not brought under control you could become domineering, vindictive and even violent.

Be careful with your diet; you do enjoy your sweets. Sports are often a good outlet for a person with your drive. Remember, your talents and abilities are a gift from a higher source, which should promote gratitude and humility, rather than pride and conceit. Don't allow pride or overconfidence to become your master.

Aiming for a career of being your own boss is best for you. You do better working alone than with a group. You'll do fine in a group if you are the leader. Politics, or a being a CEO, among other things, may interest you as a career.

You can become lazy. Why? Because you do everything more quickly than everyone else and you are easily bored. Use that energy to investigate and achieve on your own. Or just chill out and get out into nature and smell the roses.

Taking charge, stepping out of the box, and risking it all on a new venture, is what excites you.

Prolific actor, Jack Nicholson, is a Life Path 1, and what I just described above is the perfect persona of Nicholson. Always seen with the sunglasses, needing to be noticed, always with a young beautiful woman, needing to stand out. Need I say more?

KEY WORDS for Life Path 1

It's all about me! Idea person; leadership qualities.

Number (2)

YOU ARE SENSITIVE perceptive, patient and shy. These qualities are both your strengths and weaknesses, although you possess enormous sensitivity to your feelings and those of others, that same sensitivity can cause you to hold back and suppress your talents. Your awareness, diplomatic skills, and organizational talents allow you the ability to complete difficult tasks that others don't even consider doing.

Many counselors, nurses, massage therapists, teachers, and caregivers are born under a Life Path 2. You are a team player, and you make an excellent partner. You don't like to stand in the forefront; you are the power behind the throne. You are in love with love. You will do anything to avoid confrontation. You're a lover; not a fighter. You are a very cooperative, patient person.

You have the ability to tap into your intuition and know what people want, or feel. You work well with groups and somehow always find a way to create harmony among diverse opinions.

You enjoy music and poetry and require a harmonious environment. You have an eye for beauty and a fine sense of balance and rhythm. You have healing capabilities, especially in the field of healing modalities.

You should work in a profession that you really love because money is secondary to you; it's almost like the money is your reward for doing what you really love. Meaning you will not be happy taking a job just to make large amounts of money.

You are a sensitive and passionate lover; your perceptiveness makes you aware of your partner's needs and desires, which you are able to fulfill. However, if you are mistreated or jilted you can have a wicked tongue, to the point of hurting others more than they hurt you.

Jennifer Aniston is a Life Path 2. The American actress, director, producer, and businesswoman is the daughter of actor John Aniston and actress Nancy Dow. Her marriage to Brad Pitt hailed the couple as having the love of a lifetime. Fortunately, because she so believes in love, Aniston's marriage to Justin Paul Theroux, an American actor, director, and screenwriter seems to have the same "flavor" for a lover of love.

How sweet she is; Aniston definitely is someone who avoids confrontation and she truly loves love. You can see it in her eyes.

KEY WORDS for Life Path 2 is:

Peacemaker. Shy, power behind the power.

Number (3)

YOU POSSESS A talent for creativity and self-expression. Many writers, poets, actors, comedians, singers, broadcasters, counselors and musicians are born under the 3 Life Path. You are witty, possess a gift for gab, and savor the limelight, and you are the communicators of the world. You have a charismatic personality, and are a great listener. You have no issue in putting yourself out there. Your talent for the expressive arts is so strong that you may have felt it tugging at you at a very young age. You enjoy being the life of the party. Your artistic abilities can only be developed, however, through discipline and commitment to your talents. Commitment, concentration and hard work are the only means of to bring forth your talents. This is difficult for 3's because they want to live life in the moment and allow themselves to think, Tomorrow will take care of itself!

Your creativity is the gift that can give you the comfort and luxury you desire, but not without continual focus and discipline. You could easily squander your talents by becoming a social butterfly and not being serious with your gifts. This is because you live for today and don't worry about tomorrow. You are optimistic and possess resilience when encountering setbacks. You are socially active, popular, and an inspiration to others. You tend to look on the bright side of everything.

You can be generous to a fault. You may have difficulty handling money because you can be disorganized and not particularly serious about your responsibilities. You must watch your finances. You too easily spend without thinking of tomorrow. You are also noticed for your pretty eyes and round faces, just like cherubims... beautiful and angelic.

You are emotional and vulnerable; when hurt, you withdraw. Everyone needs to get away from when you get in a mood because everyone will feel it. Then when you're over the "moment" you'll come back like it never happened. You'll be sarcastic in a joking manner, but won't quite understand why everyone thinks you're perhaps nuts. You are very restless and always need to be on the move. When you use your skills positively, you are a force for good in the world by uplifting others, in turn bringing success and happiness into your life. Your life is a stage and you are the main character.

John Travolta is a Life Path 3. He loves the limelight, but when he's hurt he withdraws, a trait we have seen throughout his career. There have been times when John Travolta was just not around. For a time, you heard nothing about him, but he bounced back with a great movie. And what about his eyes! Travolta also played an unconventional angel in the movie Michael, which often referred to his eyes.

KEY WORDS for Life Path 3:

I live for today. Communicator, lover.

Number (4)

YOU ARE PRACTICAL and down-to-earth, with strong ideas about right and wrong. You like things in your life to be organized and under control. You do things in order—and step by step. Once you make a commitment to learn something—or do something—you're in the game, so to speak, until you master it or get it done. Bankers, financial planners, architects, and landscapers, are born under the 4 Life Path.

Hard work is your mantra. You don't get into any get-rich-quick-schemes. You have the ability to overcome limitations or blocks because you are good at dismantling all manner of things and then reconstructing them. You are a natural builder of things, which includes being a lover and builder of a family unit.

Strong foundations are necessary for you and you have the ability to create them. You are spiritual, and security in your life is very important as well as your finances. You're all about justice and honor and yet at times you're quick to judge others. You are a very dependable and honest person. You enjoy doing things in and for your community to make it a better place to live.

You are loyal to those you love. You don't take issue with being in a team, or on a team, but the rules must be laid out and defined in order for you to do your best.

You have to be careful not to be bossy and rude. You need to be disciplined to persevere, which means you must keep your eye on the ball.

You can handle money quite well. Whatever amount you make, you like to save some for a rainy day. You need to feel secure in order to excel and focus on your journey. You don't embrace change. Once things are functioning comfortably for you, you resist change. You can be too cautious when changes are necessary, which can cause you to miss opportunities that present themselves.

You are well suited for marriage and often become a responsible, loving, parent. However, anything that violates your profound sense of order, such as separation or divorce, can be a shattering and devastating experience for you. You can have an obsessive nature and even vengeful, seeking justice. On the other hand you are a true survivor.

No one can lie to a 4; you will pick up on it and call them out. You will forgive them, but you will never trust them again.

Bill Gates is a Life Path 4. Now who is more level headed and organized, and passionate to build a strong foundation for his life and for others around him? He and his wife Melinda run a foundation, "A Call for Global Citizenship". What better way for Bill Gates to show he is the epitome of a foundation builder for and with love?

KEY WORDS for Life Path 4:

Foundation builder; seeker of truth. Money for security.

Number (5)

YOU ARE ALL about freedom. You are by nature an investigator. Adventure is what you're all about. You bore easily; you have energy and ideas that makes others just scared to be around you. You are a mover and a shaker. If you are not experiencing this kind of life you must have very subtle Core numbers. You enjoy travel, thinking outside the box and you often wonder why others don't get things that just come naturally to you. You have no patience; you can't handle wasting time. Your life is truly a roller coaster ride. You should not marry young. If you marry before the age of 27 it may not last, unless your partner's natural numbers match with yours. Public relations, sales, advertising, and law enforcement people are born under the 5 Life Path.

You need three life cycles of experience and wisdom before you are ready to commit. If you commit to a relationship before you experience three life cycles, being with another 5 who is someone who gets you is a must to successfully stay in the relationship. If not, you will be miserable. But later in life, once you commit—good or bad—you're in it for life, especially if your partner provides you with the finer things in life you enjoy.

You're willing to work for the things you want and enjoy, but you'll also readily accept them if "given" to you. You need to be your own boss... you'll listen to advice, but you can't take orders. If you have a 9 to 5 job (which is almost impossible for a 5), and you want to get up and go and your boss says, "No," you're so gone! You enjoy variety in your life, and you are as curious as a cat. You enjoy investigating and getting your own answers; therefore you possess excellent research skills. You want to know everything and you want to experience everything in life. You are a multi-tasker. You can be an excellent motivational speaker.

The thing is, you must learn to focus and discipline yourself. You are so full of ideas that if things don't happen quickly enough you'll drop a project and move on to the next idea. Unfortunately, the idea you dropped could have been the one to have ultimately led you to the desired finer life you so crave. This is why having a compatible match makes your life easier;

otherwise, you bore easily and are always on to the next idea that pops into your head.

If you can't make your next idea happen quickly enough, you might experience addictive behavior patterns, such as drugs, alcohol, sex, or food, just to escape the reality of not living the life you desire. You may also lack discipline and structure, but still want the best of the best, and can become cranky when you don't have what you want.

Steven Spielberg is a Life Path 5. Look what he created for the world with all his ideas! He obviously is disciplined, and loves adventure, which shows in his movies. He uses his discipline, research, and investigative skills, to put his ideas into action. Do you think he's bored? I think not—not with the fine life he is enjoying because of his work.

KEY WORDS for Life Path 5

I just want to be free. Natural investigator, impatient

Number(6)

We accept the love we think we deserve.

~ Stephen Chbosky
American novelist, screenwriter, and film director.

YOU ARE THE lover, the fixer, the problem solver, and the caretaker. You will sacrifice yourself to help someone in need, especially if they are your family or loved ones you consider family. In return the 6 enjoys being rewarded (for a lack of a better word) in kind. You also enjoy the finer things in life, and will flaunt it. You are very loyal, and like a magnet you also have the ability to draw unto you whatever you desire.

When you get cranky, everyone around you feels it, and they just have to get away from you. But when it's over, it's over. You try to make a joke to let everyone know it's over and things are now back to normal (whatever normal is for you). Sometimes others just don't get what the issue was in the first place, but because you are so loveable and loved by those around you, they will let it go. Drama is part of the 6 personality; you will do anything for anyone, but if you don't get your way in the end, watch out!

You enjoy a nice car, pretty home and fine clothes and you like to get dressed up and be noticed. You are, or can be, an excellent parent. That doesn't mean the kids will respond the way you want them to, but you will always do your best and you will do it from a place of love. Mechanics, engineers, and home-based work people are born under the sign of a 6 Life Path.

You always want to extend yourself to others. Your need to fix everything; making everything all right is what you are all about. If things are going smoothly, you are capable of creating an incident surrounded by drama just so you can fix it. You also don't mind giving until it hurts because you do expect a return in kind.

Goldie Hawn is a Life Path 6. An American actress, director, and producer, she is well known for television and film appearances. Every time you see a photo of Goldie she is dressed up and with family; she shows her family off. She is magnetic and people are just drawn to her innocent smile and those eyes, well... you gotta love those eyes. She's a lover in every sense of the word. Her career began with a TV sitcom, Laugh In. Look it up and see how she looked and acted... and tell me she's not a class 6!

KEY WORDS for Life Path 6

Love is the answer. Self sacrificing, drama

Number (7)

All spiritual practice is the art of shifting perspectives.

~ Teal Swan (1984 -) Author and New Age Leader

THIS IS THE highest number of spirituality. You must seek higher truth; you must learn the answers to your existence. You seek truth in all you do. You also are someone who, in a crowd, will act like you're not paying attention, but the joke is on them because you take it all in.

You are slow to warm because you want to make sure to whom you give your attention and time. You are never lonely when you are alone; you actually enjoy your alone time. Woefully, the 7 people stay in their heads too much and must learn how to get out of "there" before they drive themselves nuts by over analyzing things.

Mathematics, religious calling, chemistry, and science are some talents the 7 Life Path is born with.

You actually have the talent and ability to be a good writer. You might also seriously consider writing because when you stay in your head you tend to lack details, which requires you to ask for help. Asking someone to work with you on the details is good for you. Then you can get those ideas and thoughts out, and implement your plan.

Be aware of emptiness in your life. There is a part of you that desires close companionship. When you don't have the companionship in your life you desire, it can lead to isolation and you can become cynical or suspicious, develop hidden and selfish agendas, and become too withdrawn and independent. These things will shut you down from experiencing the true joy of friendship, companionship and love.

You must also guard yourself against feeling you are the center of the universe. It is your challenge in life to maintain your independence without feeling isolated or superior. You must hold fast to your unique view of the world, while at the same time remain open to others and the knowledge they have to offer. You are very intuitive as well; pay attention to your gut.

Stephen Hawking has 7 and is the epitome of his Life Path number: A problem-solving dreamer, Hawking was born in Oxford, England in 1942. Early in life he showed a high passion for science and cosmology. Unfortunately, he was diagnosed with amyotrophic lateral sclerosis at age 21.

Not to be deterred by a debilitating illness, Hawking completed groundbreaking work in physics and cosmology. His writing has helped make higher-level science understandable and assessable to many others.

KEY WORDS for Life Path 7

Why am I here; what is my purpose? Writer, Intuitive.

Number (8)

Money and success don't change people; it merely amplifies what they already are.

~ Will Smith
American actor, producer, rapper, and songwriter.

THE MOST MISUNDERSTOOD number in all Life Paths, the 8 is the late bloomer. Because your mind says, "One day at a time, one step at a time... I will get there!" And get there you will. Once in motion, you just keep going. Even if you lose track of time, or some obstacle gets in the way—it really doesn't matter to you; you are confident that you have the ability to get it all. Even if you lose it you know you can get it back, and even exceed what you already accomplished. This is the number of success and money and intellect.

The 8 does nothing in a small way. The best career—if your Core numbers have more than one 8—is business. Own it, control it, manage it, and make money. Very smart are the 8's; they also genuinely want to do good for mankind, but know it takes money, so there are no limits to what an 8 can accomplish.

Some other vocations for an 8 would be law enforcement, upper management, accountant, or financial advisor. As an 8, when you embrace the spiritual side, you become masters and leaders; you take charge and authority. You do delegate and give your ideas to others to get it done.

Your life lesson is to learn there is, and can be; a balance between your spiritual and material worlds and you can be comfortable with both. The reason is…8 is the number of karma, which gives you great intuition and spirituality. If you put the 8 on its side it is the symbol of infinity. Therefore the 8's possess infinite possibilities.

The negative side of 8 is you're not getting the money, business and success… because it wasn't meant for you. You tend to blame someone or something for your lack. This, of course, is not true. You are the orchestrator of your life. You must also learn that being a good financial provider for your family is not the only way to show love. This 8 wants you to learn what really matters; bad choices and dishonesty from a prior lifetime may present themselves in this life. You may even experience a recurring pattern of people entering and leaving your life, and returning again. You are reviewing lessons you brought with you from prior lifetimes. There may also be times where your direct honesty may be hard to take. You also have a strong desire to be recognized for your achievements.

Elizabeth Taylor was a Life Path 8. I feel compelled to ask, "Need I say more?" However, it is best to give voice to a beautiful and spiritual woman we all came to know and love, as one of the greatest screen actresses to blossom during Hollywood's Golden Age. It may be difficult to ascertain whether Taylor was most famous for myriad marriages, exquisite jewelry, or those stunning violet eyes. Taylor delivered riveting performances; that fame was ultimately touched by tragedy and loss, but grounded in a focus on philanthropy. Perhaps her son Michael Wilding's statement best summarizes her amazing life:

My mother was an extraordinary woman who lived life to the fullest, with great passion, humor, and love ... We will always be inspired by her enduring contribution to our world.

KEY WORDS for Life Path 8

Do as I say, not as I do. Intellect, confidence, late bloomer, and money number.

Number(9)

True leaders don't create followers...they create more leaders!

~ J. Sakiya Sandifer
Songwriter, author, and Founder of the Think Movement

NATURAL HUMANITARIANS AND true leaders, the 9 Life Path encompasses 1 through 8. This is the universal number of love, eternity, and faith. This is also the number of service to humanity, and the light worker or the enlightened one. This number will lead by example.

Key words for this Life Path number include: self-sacrifice, selfless, generous, romantic, inner-strength, intuitive, strength of character, public relations, and responsibility.

The 9 is frequently referred to as the "Mother Theresa number," not only because it was her Life Path number, but because 9's are particularly affected by the general welfare of others. They need to fix everything; they are either the pied piper leading the way, or the one who feels responsible for everything, especially regarding family dynamics. Those blessed with having a Life Path of 9 also make excellent coaches and social workers, and they enjoy expressing themselves through visual arts and music.

They also enjoy being interior designers landscape artist, photographer, politician, lawyer, judge, minister, teacher, healer; basically any field that requires self-sacrifice and that will have a social impact. You are often disappointed by the realities of life: the shortcomings of others, or of yourself.

Your drive to make the world a better place is what you're all about. You seem to acquire money in your life through strange and unusual ways without even pursuing it. You attract people from all walks of life, you are respected and your peers will elevate you to a position of power, not because you asked for it, but because you are someone to follow, as a true leader and lover of humanity. You do reach a point, that if you continue to help others and they don't learn to help themselves, you will cut them loose. Why? Intuitively, you know people will just lean on you because they know you will just do it for them.

Robin Williams was a Life Path 9. He tried to fix everything, but unfortunately, in the end he couldn't even fix himself. Williams truly carried the weight of the world on his shoulders until he broke, but what a wonderful man he was!

Williams, born in 1951, was the great-great grandson of a Mississippi Governor and Senator. His parents were also prominent and successful, thus it was not surprising the actor first studied political science before finding his real place in theatre at Juilliard. The heart and soul of his wild comic talent allowed Williams to be extremely effective and successful with the improvisation that both brought ire to his directors, and an Academy Award for his dramatic skills.

Chapter 9: If You Born On The 4. (Fourth) Or 13th (Thirteen), Or 22nd (Twenty Second) Or 31st (Thirty First) Of Any Month Than Kindly Read The Following:

THE NUMBER FOURS

In general those with a birth date of four are called the "salt of the earth". Loyal, productive, earnest, Fours love home, family, and country. They prefer secure environments and stability. They take a cautious approach and enjoy working with their hands. They are builders and managers. While Fours are traditionalist they are also enthusiastic supporters of measure that result in reform, improvement and efficiency. You succeed through business, management, production, and anything connected to building and the earth. You learn things the hard way and have confidence that you can learn anything if shown the principles.

You may have trouble seeing the "big picture". You can be very cautious and careful in approach to work and life in general. You must make an effort to keep up to date. With fundamentals no frill thinking you have strong ideas about the right way to do things. You may work on several manual jobs in your life before working your way up to a position where your experience is respected. You make you a better manager and organizer. You may be more responsible and self-disciplined. Sincere and honest, you are a serious and hardworking individual.

Your feelings are likely to seem somewhat repressed at times. You have on your ability to show and express affections, as feeling are very closely regulated and controlled.

For number four natives there is a good deal of rigidity and stubbornness associated with them as they happen to be

Powerful, builder, egocentric, and unpredictable. Non-conforming, strong, hard to keep up with energetically. Very mental, hard to grasp, like relating through a smokescreen, evasive. Good sense of order, keen observation skills. You radiate reliability and consistency. People trust you and feel secure with your judgment.

You are seen as a cornerstone of a business, and are relied upon to do you work efficiently and expertly. You have strength and respectability. You tend to dress in a utilitarian manner, concerned mostly with convention, practicality, durability, Reliability Consistency and price. You present yourself as someone who values correctness, control, and precision. You want to be judged on the basis of your performance, rather Minor Personality .You are frugal and have learned to respect the dollar. You are concerned about the security of your future and those you love; however, this may appear to others as a bit too austere.

IF YOU WERE BORN ON THE 13th

You do well in business involved with manufacturing commerce real estate and building (especially remodeling). You are more capable of verbal expression then those born on the 4th and possess creative ability that absorb you. You would like to be more socially successful, find a great deal of satisfaction in your work. You have an exceptional ability to reform and improve any situation or condition. You may have strong emotional nature that erupts suddenly because you have tendency to ignore your feelings.

You have excellent concentration. Your discipline comes to rely upon you. You can work hard; need be careful not to become overworked to the point that you no longer take time to waste. Yet you may feel that you have to find the work that you truly would love to do or were meant for you. Your challenge is to make the most of what you are. There may be a feeling that your talents are buried. This can lead to try many different vocations and you may try to find some alternative against all odds. Your co-workers recognize your discipline and come to rely upon you. Your challenge is to make the most of what you are doing right now. Using your considerable perseverance and determination. You need to raise the work you are currently responsible for to a high value of favorable result.

You would also need to cultivate faith and a willingness to apply yourself to the in order to develop such an attitude, or else you may wander from job to job, relationship to relationship friendship to friendship. You can be stubborn and rigid, and this can, and lead to frustration and depression for you. Things seem to take to reciprocation, especially when you resist bringing fresh approaches into your unique ways of doing things.

The ways to your success are your willingness to discipline in your life, and make the most of every opportunity that comes your way in terms of being a winner and a successful person. You have a great love for your family, its tradition and the community. You are the architect of any work you commit to, you get your work done with great zeal and accuracy.

You possess a considerable amount of talent and are always looking for some solid form of expression. Your subordinates get impressed with your discipline and come to trust on you. You may feel that you have yet to found the work you truly love to do.

You may also have a feeling that at times your talents are buried in depth and it becomes difficult for you to find them and your challenge would be to make the most of it to search and find them.

The nature is guiding you. You need to make a habit of faith and apply yourself to the matter when at work. If you refuse to develop such an habit, you may wander from job to job, relationship to relationship and friendship to friendship.

Your positive qualities: initiative ambition, creativity, independence, self-expression, love of freedom. Your negative nature:

unemotional, rebelliousness impulsiveness, indecision, bossism, and at times cruelty.

IF YOU WERE BORN ON THE 22nd

This minister number requires you to work for the universal good rather than for personal ambition. This means that spiritual study should be a large part of your education. You are competent at almost anything you undertake.

You will find that your varied experience will someday be appropriate in a very challenging project. Your work must meet your ideals; you may pursue a hobby because you feel it will eventually pay off. You are not interested in status or luxury, but in making a significant contribution and living your life in a meaningful manner.

You will recognize a special quality in others. You are subject to a good deal of nervous tension. You can be single minded and realize your power is channeled from above. You are sensitive, analytical, and capable of handling large scale undertakings, with immense power to judge and having the capacity of assuming of working long and hard towards their completion.

Especially in your early years of your life, there is rigidity or stubbornness in you, and you tend to hide that feeling. Idealistically, you work for the greater cause with a good deal of inner strength and power within you. You have the qualities of an orderly and patient fellow. You can easily approach a problem methodically and systematically and can solve it without much difficulty.

You are very aware and intuitive powers within you. You possess the capacity to start your enterprise small and take practical steps toward enlarging it to its full scope. For greater strength, you can be deeply afraid of the dimensions of your ambitions. If your challenge is to be done willing you have a gift for seeing both the details of a plan and how it should be unfolded although you may secretly feel that nothing will measure up to your original dream.

You have a strange character. You like both good and bad. But the evil elements in bad attract you more. Therefore, you will look for special opportunities to drift into evil ways. With this subsequently, you can turn away from your goal and ambitions and this results in sad result with disappointment knocking at resulting in the sacrifice of your dream because of fear of failure.

Your solutions tend to be unique. You have good talents to make money. You keep your own counsel and have much inner strength. You will win in competitions, races, gambling, and other speculative games. On the other hand you can be nervous and suffer grave doubts about yourself, which you also tend to hide from others. Making it possibility that you will be surrounded by people who wait for exploiting your weakness.

Therefore, you need to be more careful even with your near and dear. You have to keep a constant watch over your friends too. Any one of them or a group of these persons can cheat you. You need to work for the universal good rather than for personal ambition. This means that the spiritual study in you should be, in greater part of your career. You are competent at almost anything you undertake. You will find that your varied experience will someday be appropriate in a very challenging project. Your work must meet your ideals with which you may pursue a hobby because you feel it will eventually pay off.

You are not interested in status or luxury, but in making a significant contribution and living your life in a meaningful manner. You may have many friends. You will recognize a special quality in others. Your number as twenty-two will also display originality, competence and reformative abilities. You can be single minded and serious and need to feel in control. You must realize your power is channeled from above. You are sensitive, analytic, and judgmental.

Due to the intense vibration people with number twenty two as their birth no are born to get the sense of obligation in life and purity of consciousness. Quite often they tend to face amazing events have challenging years of early life, yet they often lead extraordinary lives after learning to utilize their full potential.

Positive qualities: master builder. Great accomplisher. Unique qualities unorthodox approach to problem solving. Strong leader, can in a positive vein, you possess practical approach, idealist, development inner strength is charisma to attract athe world.

Negative Traits: negative expression unorthodox methods, eccentricity. Dominating at times confused and over commanding.

IF YOU WERE BORN ON THE 31st

You derive great satisfaction from working with your hands and may be a sculptor or painter. You may have very high ambition for yourself. You are very traditional love your friends and remember their birthdays.

You may be a great cook. You love to travel and socialize, but work for extremely long hours if motivated. You do not enjoy living alone and will take on solicitous attitude towards your mate. You love talk about yourself and your plans and expected others to be interested. You are an excellent care taker organizer and manager. You have a great love for your community. You would follow family tradition and community rules. You are the foundation stone of any enterprise. You are dependable and quite an energetic worker. You possess a good amount of talent that is searching for concrete forms of expression. You can work hard, long and continuously. As long as you tend to take good care of yourself, you have excellent power of concentration and vision.

You love travel and don't like to live alone. For this you should marry quite early for the sake of responsibility and stability. You being practical thinker with strong imagination you often show success in the business matter. Being sincere and serious you possess, patience and determination necessary to accomplish great heights. The keys to your success are your willingness and your sincere hard work.

Your fellows recognize your discipline and come to trust and rely upon you in order to maintain order and discipline in their life, and for the most opportunities that come in their lives. Basically, you may feel that you have yet to find the work you truly love or were meant to do.

There may be a feeling that your talents are buried too deep for you to find them. This can lead you to try many different vocations without a feeling that you have truly found your place. The stars and this universe guide you always. But you need to cultivate faith and willingness in yourself. If you refuse to develop such an attitude, you may wander from place to place, job to job, friendship to friendship relationship to relationship. Therefore you must use your considerable perseverance and determination.

You do not care about materialistic possessions or gains, about the money losses or the superficial profits; it's the freedom of speech and action that you care most. Freedom to do all things at will is your main desire.

Number 31 are the people who act according to their own will and heart, and they happen not get into any sort of thing which acts against their mental happiness even if the all the thing are of good lucrative attraction. They enjoy deep research and studies of human psychology, Astrology, religious scriptures and occult sciences. If the natives of number 31 do not care for the good vibrating number matching their birth no and keep any name accordingly to their wish and will they are likely to lead a goalless wanderlust, Vagabond life. In this way, they are become the real rebels in their own society who defy the traditions and social practices. Even if success comes on their way, they don't cherish it or embrace it with passion but to the contrary, they will nonattached and uninterested. Hence forth non matching number should be avoided in their own interest.

Their skill will help them to raise their own status in life and with this unique skill they would be helping the people by knowledge of scriptures, science and mathematics. They desire to be as free, as a bird and so they do not like to live under the control of others.

They know something about everything. They will express their ideas bluntly through speech and writing. People will seek their advice.

They are prone to lust and they often visit various places for the sake of gathering the knowledge of competitive skill. In this way, they enrich themselves with wide experience. During a conversation, they will wait till the other person completes his speech but will tend to interfere.

When provoked and they become angry at once. But as they grow older with the year to come, they will gather some experience and will improve themselves. Whatever it may be, they are not deterred by worries. For a short while they may feel sad but soon they will drive out the shady thoughts.

Natives having number 31 as their number have high nervous power. They are quite tall and their looks are majestic. They have good power of wisdom and talented thoughts. They are seen helping others and with all these qualities they are praised by one and all. If anyone sheds tears narrating his difficulty, these people feel proud in joining him. They have an extremely sharp brain and are capable of replying at lightning speed. They are welcomed everywhere. They would not become addicted to any bad habit.

Even if they happen to get into this, they have the power to give it up soon.

They would strain themselves to collect and earn and money. But when they want to spend it, with a merry heart their tension starts and this leads to unhappiness. When alone, they will feel sorry for their spending and extravagance. Though they are mentally bold yet they are stubborn and rigid. This behavior can, often, lead to frustration and repression for them. Things seem to take for better especially when they leave their rigidity.

It is generally not good if your name number does not contribute to find worldly enjoyments or worldly success. This will lead you to be a poor husband or parent.

You must examine your name properly to see if it does contain any bad alphabet. Bad combination of alphabets in your number can cause you loss, defamation, and accidents. Hence forth the power of numbers advises you to avoid negative numerology in your name.

Positive Traits: quite tall and their looks are majestic master builder scale solving. Strong leader, well practical approach, the idealist, charisma to attract.

Negative Traits: stubborn and rigid, undertakings unorthodox approaches to problems, unnecessary, spending, Extravagant.

Chapter 10: Comparisons To Astrology

Many people who study numerology have a kind of negative concept of astrology. And the same can be said for astrologists. When you believe in a system, like astrology or numerology, it can be hard to understand or accept other systems. However, if you begin to look at the two systems, you'll soon begin to see that instead of contradicting each other, they actually complement each other. This shouldn't come as much as a surprise, however, since the believed founder of numerology, Pythagoras, was a mathematician and a studier of astronomy.

Before going into how astrology and numerology compare, here's a quick refresher on what the two systems are about. Numerology, as you probably know pretty well at this point, is a study of numbers and how those numbers influence and change people and their lives. Astrology is the study of how the position of stars and other celestial bodies influence relationships. While there's a lot more to be said about each system, these are the definitions that will be used for each in this section.

If you were to take a closer look at astrology and the way the charts and meanings are determined, you'll probably start to notice something. Astrology uses numbers for every single chart, from the angles between the stars and also how these angles relate to one another. If you look a little closer, you'll soon begin to see a pattern. Numbers are used throughout astrology to get a complete understanding of the charts that are used in the study. And, just like that, you begin to see the relationship between astrology and numerology.

This connection continues to even deeper levels. In astrology, the planets, sun, and moon are assigned specific numbers. It might surprise you, but those numbers just happen to be the numbers 0 – 9. Sound familiar? That's not the only place you'll see numbers in the study of astrology. The zodiac signs that are so often used and followed by dedicated astrologists are also given numbers. Once again, these numbers are 0 – 9.

So, in actuality, astrology and numerology aren't all that different. Sure, they offer different information and even use different methods to get this information. But, at the heart of it, astrology is numerology. Just like numbers are the building blocks of society, so is numerology the building blocks of astrology.

It should be noted that numerology is much more simple than astrology, both in its studies and in its readings. This might come as a deterrent for avid astrologists, but they still shouldn't overlook the importance of numerology.

To get a better understanding of how astrology and numerology correlate, try getting readings for both. When you compare them, you'll probably be shocked to see that they don't contradict or dispute each other. More than likely, you'll find a brief overview from one and a deeper look into that overview from the other. Using both will give you a certain amount of insight into yourself that you might not have gained from using just one method.

Chapter 11: Soul Number

Your soul number is made up from the vowels (a, e, i, o and u) in your full birth name. Sometimes Y (if there are no other vowels in the syllable (for example, in Lyn) is counted as a vowel and when it is preceded by a vowel and sounded as one sound (for example, in Hayden. (You might want to try the calculations both with and without a Y.) A W is treated as a vowel when it is preceded by a vowel and produces a single sound (for example, in Bradshaw).

Your soul number describes your inner self and those things you don't expose to those around you – what you prefer to keep private. It describes your greatest motivations and the qualities you want in a partner and refers to what is most dear to your heart, your inner cravings, likes and dislikes. This number often refers to the part of you that receives the least attention.

1 What makes you content: succeeding in any form of competition. Proud of your abilities, you want recognition. You are ambitious and determined and a leader. You are driven to success and a loyal friend. You prefer to look at the big picture and leave the details to others. Ambitious and determined, you operate independently. Beware of being boastful.

2 What makes you content: love and harmony in your life. Your motivation is centred on friendships, partnerships, and companionship. You want to work with others cooperatively. You can be sympathetic, concerned and devoted. You tend to be sensitive and diplomatic and are emotional. You're willing to work hard to achieve a harmonious environment. You can be sympathetic, concerned and devoted. Beware of being over-sensitive, timid or fearful.

3 What makes you content: expressing your creativity. Your desire in life is to enjoy things to their fullest. You want an active social life and enjoy a large circle of

friends. You enjoy being in the limelight. You have good communication skills and are friendly, outgoing and sociable. You don't like appreciate pointing out your faults. Beware of scattering your energy.

4 What makes you content: things staying as they are and feeling appreciated. Stability appeals to you and you don't like sudden change. Excellent at organising, you are responsible, reliable, practical, honest, sincere, and conscientious. You need to feel secure both financially and professionally. You have a large circle of friends, although you don't like anyone to point out your faults. You tend to hide your feelings. Beware of being too rigid,keywordsstubborn or narrow-minded.

5 What makes you content: a life of freedom and adventure. You're adaptable and versatile. You'd like to follow a life of freedom, excitement, adventure and unexpected events. You are an adventurer at heart. You dislike routine, and tend to jump from one thing to another. You don't

want to be tied down to a relationship, and it may be hard to commit to one person. Beware of being superficial or irresponsible.

6 What makes you content: your family. You'd like to be appreciated for your ability to handle responsibility. Friendship, love, and affection are high on your list of priorities. You have diplomatic tendencies and like working with people rather than by yourself. It is important for you to have a harmonious environment. You have a huge capacity for responsibility and are ready to assume more than your share of the load. Often, you are known for your generosity, understanding and sympathetic attitude. You like to help people and are creative. Be careful that people don't take advantage of you. Beware of being over emotional or resentful.

7 What makes you content: spending time alone dreaming. Laid back and withdrawn, you can be timid around people you don't know and find it hard to handle social

situations. You may be too laid back and withdrawn to succeed in business. You enjoy your own company and like time to think about the world around you. You are timid around people you don't know well and social situations can be strained. You feel fulfilled by seeking wisdom. Beware of becoming isolated.

8 What makes you content: feeling powerful. Power, status and success are very important to you. You rarely let your emotions cloud your judgment. You are an organiser at heart, and a leader, not a follower. As you like to supervise and organise, you can be successful in the commercial world. You have an analytical mind and good judgement, and are a good judge of character. Self-controlled, you rarely let emotions cloud judgment. Beware of being domineering, rigid or stubborn.

9 What makes you content: doing something that benefits humanity. You want to give to others and are highly motivated to give friendship and affection.

You are sympathetic and generous and able to view life in broad terms. You often express high ideals and an inspirational approach. You can be self-sacrificing. Beware of being over sensitive and resentful.

11 What makes you content: sharing your ideas. Much of your thinking relates to the abstract and the spiritual. You dream of the perfect world and are idealistic. You are devoted to your beliefs and are good at handling higher, more abstract forms of thought. You are not very practical and may have fixed ideas of right and wrong. Beware of nervous tension.

22 What makes you content: feeling that you have made a contribution. Much of your thinking relates to the abstract and the spiritual. You are motivated toward idealistic concepts, and sharing your ideas. You have a broad outlook and are highly practical. You have an innate desire to express your power you feel in a concrete manner and want to make a considerable contribution to the world. With your

unusual perception and awareness, you can be extremely diplomatic. Beware of being over sensitive or impractical.

33 What makes you content: spiritually transforming the world. You value a state of grace above all else and may appear as somewhat of an enigma. People find it difficult to determine the logic behind your actions. You spend much of your time being misunderstood or persecuted for your beliefs. If you are enlightened and detached from emotions or events, the actions of ordinary people have little effect on your directive to spiritually transform the world. Beware of being unclear.

Chapter 12: Personal Day

In this chapter I shall discuss what we can use our knowledge of numerology for. Within the constraints of daily living numerology can be a useful guide for ordering one's existence. Obviously every single day is composed of a series of numbers; so the fifth of February 2013 becomes 05/02/2013. Now when these numbers are added together they make thirteen and taken down to a single number this makes four. So this day is a four day.

Now for personal use you need to take your destiny number, which is the number you get from adding together your birth date, and add that to the day number. This will give you your personal day number. For instance, my destiny number is two and if I add that to the day number of four, it makes my personal day number six. Because of the different vibrations of each number it stands to reason that different activities will be better performed on certain days rather than others.

Personal Day Number One – This is a great day for new beginnings. Anything project that needs starting should be done today; this is often a high energy day and it is a great day for thinking up lots of new ideas. It's quite possible that there will not be enough time to finish every thing so it might be as well to write down a lot of these new ideas so that you can finish them off at a later date. This will also be a good day to show yourself off in a good light. If you have an audition on this day, the chances are that it will go well. The number one is ruled by the sun and so this is a good day to shine.

Personal Day Number Two – This is a good day to look after anything. Whether it is a sick cat or a stressed child the chances are that this is a day when everyone will be comforted, including yourself. Even if you just give yourself an extra long soak in the bath, it will bring you much needed solace. You will be sensitive to people's moods and needs today and so will be able to know what they want before they do. This is unlikely to be a day of arguments; it is much more likely to be a day of gentleness.

Personal Day Number Three – This is a great day to get out and explore the world around you. You would particularly enjoy going somewhere you've never been before. If you can't get out of the house then you can use this day as an opportunity to read about a new philosophy or religion. This is also a good day to have fun doing something you've never done before. It's all about going to places, either mentally, physically or spiritually that you've never been to before.

Personal Day Number Four – This is a work day. This will never be a good day for goofing off. But it will be a perfect day to get all those little jobs done that you've been putting off for ages. Anything that demands a lot of detailed work will prosper today so go through the fine print. This can be quite a routine and boring day but it will always be a profitable one.

Personal Day Five — This is a day to communicate so pick up the phone and call all those people you've been meaning to ring for ages. Write, e-mail or phone but make sure that you get in touch. Everybody will be hanging on your every word today. This is a great day for selling things because your powers of persuasion are enhanced. If you have to do any public speaking, try to schedule it for a five day and then everything will go really well. It's also a good day to work on your personal image because that is another way of communicating, so get your hair done or buy new clothes.

Personal Day Six — This is a great day to beautify yourself or your home or even your office. It's also a great day to buy art or to draw and paint because your eye for colour and your taste will be impeccable. All this makes it another good day to shop for clothes or shoes or bags. It's a great day to make peace with people that you may have been having disagreements with because six is the number of harmony. Meetings should go smoothly and everyone should be on their best behaviour.

Personal Day Seven – This would be a great day to go on a spiritual retreat or just to do meditation and yoga. If possible today should be spent in a state of slight withdrawal from the world so that you can focus better on your spiritual journey. Obviously, this may not be possible so try to spend even a few minutes in meditation or just in a state of spiritual awareness. It is easy to make progress on any spiritual quests today so reading and study on these matters could be profitable.

Personal Day Eight – This is a great day to win. If you have to compete in business or in sport then this will be a day where victory will be more likely. Your strength and endurance will be enhanced and mentally you'll be particularly sharp. Just be careful of outbursts of temper if things don't go your way because a tantrum today will not be a small one. If you get mad everybody is likely to know about it and remember it for a long time.

Personal Day Nine – Today is a good day for finishing things and wrapping all those odds and ends up so that tomorrow you can start something new. It's also a good day to take risks as long as they are calculated, rather than foolish risks. This is a day of endings so finish that book you've been reading and watch the end of that series. If you're interested in anything to do with death then this is the day to indulge your morbid side. Visit that cemetery, indulge your gothic side; today is the day to venture into the dark.

Chapter 13: Master Numbers

The traditional master numbers are 22 and 11 but along the way, other numbers such as 33, 44, 55 and 66 were added to the list. However, there is no recorded practical use of master numbers beyond 33 so use only 11, 22, and 33 in your calculations. Don't get confused by this master number concept and when you come across them in your reading, just think of them as strengthened versions of the single core numbers in the numerological chart. It's good for you to realize that all numbers are completely equal in terms of their potential influence on humans. It is just that the number's distinct energies are manifested in special ways among different individuals.

There are three different reactions associated with the realization that you are a 'master' and in most cases, the reactions are not desirable at all. You might come across individuals with the latter group of master numbers who may think that they are superior to the earlier 'masters' and way better than all single digits in the chart because not everyone has their numbers. There is also a popular misconception that higher numbers have more potential than lower numbers. These conceptions are not rational at all and should not bother you in any way. This ego attached to master number is only a way of thinking that dwells on the negative rather than positive thinking. If the letters in your names or date of birth sums up to one of the master numbers 22, 11, or 33 ensure you contain your excitement and pride and try to be modest focusing more on the final single digit corresponding to your number. Just because your calculations say you are a 'master' doesn't mean you idle around and wait for greatness to find you. Look at the core numbers in order to understand your personality, strengths, weakness, your purpose and evaluate the effort you need put to achieve greatness. Avoid inflating your ego thinking that you are better than the rest who don't fall under this category.

On the other hand, upon realizing that your destiny number or life Path number is one of the master numbers, you can be scared or intimidated. Unaware of what to do with this naturally bestowed great "gift", you can become confused and paranoid which is also not healthy. Just refer to your core number and don't overwhelm yourself with the desire to live up to the ascribed greatness. Take a step at a time and with effort and determination, you will attain your inner potential.

Chapter 14: Virgo's Cosmic Clock

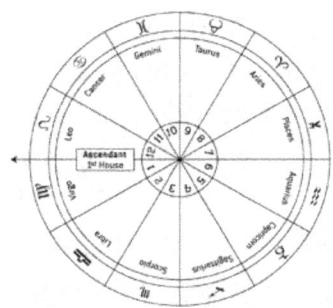

The role of the Cosmic Clock is to show the monthly position of the sun in the Zodiac and its expected influence on Virgo. For example: a Virgo who feels overwhelmed and pressured at work in June will find in the Cosmic Clock that the reason for this is the sun in the 10th house in the sign of Gemini. However, Virgo will feel relief in July, when the sun moves into Cancer, the 11th house.

The Monthly Forecast

Virgo
 Libra
 Scorpio

Sagittarius Capricorn Aquarius Pisces
Aries
Taurus
Gemini
Cancer
Leo

August 23 – September 22 September 23 – October 22 October 23 – November 21 November 22 – December 20 December 21 – January 20 January 21 – February 19 February 19 – March 20 March 21 – April 19

April	20	–	May	20
May	21	–	June	20
June	21	–	July	22
July	23	–	August	22

Sun in the 1st house Sun in the 2nd house
Sun in the 3rd house Sun in the 4th house
Sun in the 5th house Sun in the 6th house
Sun in the 7th house Sun in the 8th house
Sun in the 9th house Sun in the 10th house
Sun in the 11th house Sun in the 12th house

Note: For characteristics and meanings of the 12 houses of the Cosmic Clock, see chapter on the monthly forecast.

Virgo: Relationships with Other Signs

Virgo 1st house Libra 2nd house Scorpio 3rd house Sagittarius 4th house Capricorn 5th house Aquarius 6th house Pisces 7th house Aries 8th house Taurus 9th house Gemini 10th house Cancer 11th house Leo 12th house

Example: a Virgo woman will be rewarded with a surge of emotions from a Taurus man, but is liable to experience rejection and static from a Gemini.

LIBRA — SEPTEMBER 23rd to OCTOBER 22nd

Libra is the sign that represents the aspiration for harmony, esthetics, and beauty. Additional categories include the ideals of justice, proportion, objectivity, and of course, peace and partnership.

When speaking of beauty, there is no denying the fact that actress Catherine Deneuve, a Libra, is a prime example even at age 50+. She is thought to be one of the most beautiful women in the world, and her appearance is that of a characteristic Libra.

There is something about France that attracts the Venus energy of Libra. Brigitte Bardot is also an unforgettable Libra, who has displayed her feminine beauty to the world ever since Vadim's movie "And God Created Woman."

Since we began with beauty and actors, we can add Marcello Mastroianni, who loves to love women as much as women love to love him. Who can forget Fellini's famous love scene in "La Dolce Vita" in which Mastroianni appears with another well-known Libra, Anita Ekberg. Not just in show-business, Libra is also the sign of many politicians, including former Israeli Prime Minister Benjamin Netanyahu, a typical Libra as a politician and also as a man. For two years, he decided not to decide in connection with the peace process, which turned into the saga of his life. His marriage was far from quiet moderation and women caused him trouble. Relationships are not his territory, and neither is justice, in view of the numerous scandals that plagued his brief career as Prime Minister. In short, the categories of peace, marriage, justice, and court associated with Libra affected Netanyahu thoroughly and hard. Problems with partners were also among his difficulties. In the end, all abandoned him or were abandoned by him.

In contrast, Jimmy Carter, former U.S. president, is a classic Libra, having truly attempted to broker peace by means of dialogue, compromise, and harmony in many parts of the world, including the historic Camp David agreement between Anwar Sadat and Menachem Begin. Carter is a true Libra peacemaker, always making sure to remind the public during television interviews of his deep love and commitment to his wife Rosalynn and the importance of a good relationship. During his presidency, he even insisted that all single White House employees hurry up and get married. Perhaps he needed the assistance of the well-known Libra matchmaker, Helena Amram. It goes without saying that Libra is also the sign of matchmaking.

The beauty of Libra can be seen in actress Romy Schneider and actor Art Garfunkel, who appeared in the movie "Carnal Knowledge" during his time. India's Mahatma Gandhi was a Libra who once said, "There is no way to peace; peace is the way." "Give Peace a Chance" and "All You Need is Love" are well-known songs of another famous Libra by the name of John Lennon. Love and peace were a package deal with Lennon and his partner Paul McCartney. Yves Montand, also a Libra, loved to sing as well as to shake hands in the political arena.

In every Libra lies a hidden lawyer, aspiring to justice and consensus. Libra actor George C. Scott played the role of a lawyer in many of his films.

Conception of Time – Libra is connected to the past and to childhood, and time is associated with memory, perhaps somewhat painful. There could be a sense of fatalism. Time pressures could be associated with the home and the family.

Libra is tense, but he also causes tension in his immediate surroundings, particularly within the family. Time is connected with a parental image, and thus the home environment serves to bring back memories associated with this dimension.

Career and Work – Since Pisces occupies Libra's 6th house – that of work and everyday routine – Libra could experience situations of emptiness and vacuum in connection with work. There could be unemployment, serious trouble and situations in which it is impossible to break free of a particular job or person at work. Difficulties in communication and lack of information are possible. Certain instances may involve failure or dissolution of a project. There is something irrational in connection with work. In contrast, however, work focused on therapy or service, psychology, medicine, or connected with history and the past is possible. Cancer occupies the 10th house of careers.

Let's not forget that Bibi Netanyahu was elected on account of history. Jerusalem is essentially Cancer and fateful for Libra. A process of sacrifice and victimization at work as well as volunteerism are expected. Confusion, complications and feelings of totality go along with career.

Libra is also associated with partnerships, the hotel and tourism industry, law, fashion, beauty, cosmetics and toiletries, food, and insurance. Libras often become disappointed in their careers in contrast to the initial promises they project. This occurred with Margaret Thatcher and David Ben Gurion who, like Netanyahu, were forced to concede. With Pisces in the 6th house, Bruce Springsteen, Sting, Lennon and Montand successfully provided us with the Pisces dimension of Libra in the form of music as a profession. Famous fashion designers Donna Karan, Ralph Lauren, and Isaac Mizrahi were also born under the sign of Libra.

Money – Scorpio occupies the 2nd house of money, and Taurus is found in the 8th house. Therefore, the financial inclinations are especially strong; but there is transformation and a danger of fraud, in particular concerning real estate and land or inheritance in this area. There is a certain hidden criminality related to money, despite Libra's external elegance and good behavior. There could be situations of obsession and cycles of destruction and renewal with all that involves money and possessions. Libra will experience powerful financial regeneration as well as downfall and will often be swept away emotionally for an economic reason. There is no doubt that Scorpio and Taurus in the 2nd and 8th houses were influential in the appointment of Libra Meir Shitrit as Israel's Minister of Finance.

Relationships and Children – With Leo located in Libra's 11th house, there will be sudden detachments and separations in relation to love. The field of acquaintance is likely to be a group social event, or by means of an unusual or surprising means such as the computer or television. Libra is attracted to tall, intelligent, friendly, and communicative partners, and the deciding factor involves the ability to establish rapport. There may be amazing and unplanned surprises in love, including timeless affairs regardless of age or transoceanic romances. Break-ups or separations are accompanied by exaggerated dramatic emotional displays.

Libra's children will be special, unusual, creative and individualistic but also rebellious. The connection will be friendly, full of life and love, and lacking in authority, although there will be discipline. How? Ask a Libra how it's done.

Libras hate criticism, and it is difficult for them to receive it, but it exists behind their backs. There is attraction to those young in years or in spirit, individualistic, and even childlike to some degree. There could be a connection with diamonds, sports, the military, dance, or technical matters for a couple; with an emphasis on independence, straightforwardness, and immediacy.

Sexuality – A connection exists between sexuality, money, and possessions; but the sexual energy is stronger and more physical than what is displayed in outward behavior. With Libra, not only Aphrodite, but also the mythological god Eros, are expressed through Taurus in the 8th house position.

Home and Family – Capricorn occupies Libra's 4th house. Therefore, the family process, while not necessarily traditional or linked to the past or unrelenting memories, creates a rather overbearing sense of fate. The parents are difficult, and this is internalized by Libra. Changes are not made at home. There is a feeling of static sameness; that what was in the past will be in the future. This conception is far removed from Libra's intelligence, which is generally good.

There is sensitivity to the mother image. She is viewed as demanding, hard, and judgmental. The father is a friend who may be associated with a progressive occupation such as aviation, computers or technology. He may have contacts with many people and has the ability to improvise and invent.

Siblings could be connected with travel abroad, publicity, sports, education, freedom, and an indefinable feeling of aristocracy. There could be a love of animals. The relationship is warm, open, and they may even study together. Libra's siblings are a source of positive, optimistic, and free-flowing energy. Education, Communication, and Travel – Libra's thinking is broad and comprehensive with the ability to analyze, to abstract, and to generalize, along with good intuition and healthy intelligence. He can study at home or abroad and can specialize in more than one field. Libra loves to talk and communicate, has the ability to explain things, and is inclined to counsel others.

Health – There could be sensitivity in several areas, including the kidneys and urinary tract, the throat and thyroid gland, the neck, the upper back, the stomach, the intestines, and the immune system. Libra should be especially careful regarding proper nutrition.

Legal Situations – There could be a media expose involving a legal question that continues for a long period of time. A legal problem could be connected with transportation, business, siblings, the military or sports. A lawsuit may be related to the past, as well as a legal question concerning the home and family.

Mode of Dress – Youthful, sportive, and easy; there could be a fondness for hats.

Relation to the Past and the Future - The past is associated with the family and parental images, and the relationship to the past is one of criticism and harshness. The relationship future is loving, optimistic, and creative.

Religion – There is a desire for dialog and flexibility, as orthodoxy is associated with past history. There could be faith and a conception of a dichotomous world that changes according to the mood of the times and the situation. Libra connects to two religions, the commercialization of religion and the concept of the world, and changing philosophies of life indicating the need for communication and dialog.

Death – Natural, solid, with no special dramatic effects

Army – Military service for Libra is connected to relationships and even marriage. Duty positions may be associated with justice, negotiations, interpersonal contacts, balances and proportions, and work with young people. There is also an esthetic connection, with Aries occupying the 7th house.

Environment and Neighbors – There is good communication, and Libra radiates a feeling of youth, freshness, and sport. Relationships are open, candid and

friendly with neighbors, but Libra may have a tendency toward arrogance. He is perceived as aristocratic by those around him, and there is much talk of travel abroad. Libra is often inclined to give advice. Immediate surroundings are associated in some way with travel, nature, animals, and sports.
Cars — This area is also connected with relationships, particularly for Libra women. There is a desire for a beautiful sports car, preferably large, and imported personally from abroad.

Concessions, Sacrifices, Confusions, Illusions, and Places Where it is Difficult to be Objective and Rational — The location of Pisces in the 6th house is associated with feelings of sacrifice, victimization, vacuum experiences, failure, and dissolution in areas of work and everyday life. There is a sense of missing out and a probability of serious errors, unjust criticism both given and received. Mistakes, poor judgment, illusions, lost opportunities, and confusion could also appear at work in the form of addictions, dependencies, and inability to break away from something. This position is also associated with a mother figure that is obsessive, demanding, and physically or mentally ill. Pisces in the 6th house is associated with the failure of Margaret Thatcher and Bibi Netanyahu in the area of economics.

Chapter 15: How To Find Your Most Compatible/Social/ Business/ Love/Sex Partner For Life Path Number.. 1 - 9

a) NUMEROLOGICAL NUMBER COMPATIBILITY (NNC) :

a) No 1 Compatible with 2, 6, 9

b) No.2 Compatible with 1, 4, 8

c) No.3 Compatible with 5, 7, 9

d) No.4 Compatible with 2, 6, 8

e) No.5 Compatible with 3, 6, 7

f) No.6 Compatible with 1, 4, 5

g) No.7 Compatible with 3, 5, 8

h) No.8 Compatible with 2, 4, 7

i) No.9 Compatible with 1, 3, 9

Note: using the above as a guide you can measure your relationship with a person/persons when entering into a business, love etc pact at the very outset.

In this way you will be able to offset any upset.

b) ROMANCE, LOVE AND DATING WTH THE DIFFERENT LIFE PATHS:

In this brief chapter, you can glean the characteristics, habits and behavioral traits of each life path that you are enamored with. This is a guide and when love reigns supreme, all quirks and nonsense can be negligible and side-stepped and sideline. By knowing the way each life path acts, you will be better prepared when you are in Love,

Love, Romance and Dating (L/R/D) with a LP 1:

1) expect someone unique, with a different dress code and appearance and someone autoritative.

2) Expect him/her to dictate, and boldly express her/his thoughts.

3) Expect someone with a diverse palate, enjoying only the best and tasty food with possessiveness

4) Expect a dynamic dynamite, who can be commanding, demanding and yet loving

5) Expect someone who has the drive, determination and has high expectations and extremely romantic

6) Expect someone neat, tidy, fickle and sensitive.

7) Expect someone lost in his/her world, sensitive and highly ambitious.

L/D/R with Life Path 2:

1) Expect someone to pay attention to everything you do, say and even wear

2) Expect someone who is hyper-sensitive, so be-careful with negative comments

3) Expect someone who will cooperate with you and remember you are with a "master-mind" and he/she is capable of lying, deceiving and do both good or otherwise.

4) Expect someone who does not argue

5) Expect someone who is extremely patient with you, though you can be unbearable

6) Expect someone who is really sociable

7) Expext someone who is into the arts.

L/D/R with Life Path 3

1) Expect someone with creative ideas.

2) Expect a god-fearing person and honest loving.

3) Expect possessiveness

4) Expect tantrum's and mood swings

5) Expect high spirited romance.

6) Expect a fun loving person

7) Expect someone who demands security

L/D/R with a Life Path 4

1) Expect a non-dreamer

2) Expect a logical conversationalist

3) Expect someone who dreams of good food

4) Expect a hardworking, no nonsense approach

5) Expect someone with a non-descript fashion sense

6) Expect romance not in the traditional sense, and not one who displays it in the open

7) Expect someone who is quick to temper and fast to speak.

L/D/R with a Life Path 5

1) Expect someone with a rapid-fire thinking brain.

2) Expect someone with a penchant for food, clothes etc.

3) Expect a person full of charge energy

4) Expect someone who is competent in multi-tasking

5) Expect a person with the gift of the gab and creativity

6) Expect a high turbine sex and romance

7) Expect someone who wants space, freedom and cannot be shackled.

L/D/R with a Life Path 6

1) Expect a very caring person

2) Expect Him/her to be involved in other people's problems

3) Expect someone who is selective about food

4) Expect an emotionally strained and draped person

5) Expect a Highly sensitive and romantic person

6) Expect a person whose family comes first

7) Expect a person who does not mean what he/she says

L/D/R with a Life Path 7

1) Expect someone who is lost in his/her own world

2) Expect someone who cares for certain food

3) Expect someone who holds freindship uppermost

4) Expect someone extremely romantic and loves the preferences for the forbidden fruit

5) Expect someone who is hyper sensitive

6) Expect someone with only a handful of Friends

7) Expect someone with high hopes and dreams.

L/D/R with a Life Path 8

1) Expect someone who is goal-driven

2) Expect someone who is flashy in his/her dress sense

3) Expect someone who has taste for luxurious things in life

4) Expect a person who has little time for you

5) Expect someone who makes romance mechanical

6) Expect someone whose family come first

7) Expect someone who has high hopes, dream and ambitions with you

L/D/R with a Life Path 9

1) Expect someone who is highly caring (for all)

2) Expect someone who may be sharing his/her possessiveness with others

3) Expect a simple person (in everything, e.g. food, clothes etc.)

4) Expect someone who has time for everyone

5) Expect a highly religious or a romantic person

6) Expect a philathropist

7) Expect him to be very close to his mother or she to be very close to her father

Chapter 16: Parenting Traits On Basis Of Numbers

Each and every aspect of our personality is influenced by Planetary Numbers 1 to 9. Undoubtedly, parenthood is also governed by it. Let us have a glimpse of what type of parent you are or going to be.

NUMBER 1 (BORN ON 1, 10, 19, 28)

You are intellectual and you try your level best to inculcate your intellectual abilities in your kids too. You are always keen on developing leadership qualities in them. You are a dominant type and sometimes try to impose your ideas on them. Being Kind hearted and generous, you love to spend lavishly for fulfilling their desires.

You stretch your protective wings for them as and when required.

NUMBER 2 (BORN ON 2, 11, 20, 29)

You have capability to adjust according to situation and behave with your kids in a friendly way. Being a multi faceted personality, you care for overall personality development of your kids

NUMBER 3 (BORN ON 3, 12, 21, 30)

You love and appreciate discipline and expect same from your kids. You get tense soon, if something worries your kids, but have capacity to tackle their problems. You assume their academic liabilities willingly and are very keen towards educating them properly.

NUMBER 4 (BORN ON 4, 13, 22)

You are trendy and unconventional, with innovative mind, hence, like your kids to have a distinct personality with high intellectual level. You motivate them to participate in various competitions and try to nurture leadership qualities in them.

NUMBER 5 (BORN ON 5, 14, 23)

You like to work in independent capacity and take decisions on your own and willingly assume liabilities of your kids. You have a marked sense of intuition and like to protect your kids. You enjoy spending time with them.

NUMBER6 (BORN ON 6, 15, 24)

You like to live a comfortable life and are always keen on enhancing comfort level of your kids. Your aesthetic sense is keener and intend to develop refinement and marked aesthetic taste in your kids too. Due to your interest in academic and creative pursuits, your kids love to follow you. You are self disciplined and appreciate same discipline in your kids.

NUMBER 7 (BORN ON 7, 16, 25)

You are mild and adjusting in your behaviour, have patience and love to co ordinate, so your behaviour towards your kids is friendly .You try to tackle problems of your kids with a psychological bend of mind .If your kids commit some lapse, you never leak it out to others. You have marked interest in creative, aesthetic and literary pursuits, so you are in a position to guide your kids in these spheres.

NUMBER 8 (BORN ON 8,17,26)

You are assertive and dominant in your behaviour and expect disciplined behaviour from your kids. Whenever there be a need, you protect them. You have innate ability to take firm minded decisions. In case, your kids are in trouble, you contribute a lot in tackling the situation. Though you might face struggles in life, you don't let your kids suffer.

NUMBER 9 (BORN ON 9, 18, 27)

You are self dependent sort of person and capable of taking independent decisions. You like to be independent and don't look forward to support of your kids, rather you lend them protective wings. You prefer your kids to be very disciplined.

Chapter 17: Ace Of Wands

In the Ace of Wands, a hand reaches out from the infinite intelligence, as if a spiritual opportunity or offering is being made. The wand is still flowering, growing and developing. The leaves floating down with the wind signify material and spiritual progress and balance. In the distance on the left, there is a huge castle that represents the promise of what opportunities may come.

Those who fall under the influence of the Ace of Wands experience a "breakthrough moment" that inspires and motivates them at some point of their lifetime that eventually decides their course of destiny. The Ace of Wands encourages them to listen to their instincts and follow their gut. They will be offered an opportunity that shows great promise but it will be up to them to make the most of it and to take full advantage of the potential for the longer-term. It is almost like the spark that is needed to fuel a huge fire but these natives must work hard to build the fire as the spark itself is not enough to make such a large fire.

Teresa

Name Number 23

Mother Teresa was born on 26th August 1910. Her birth date makes her a Virgo with a strong sense of purpose. She is gifted with great devotion to fairness and a desire to apply her energy for the benefit of others. She is quiet and introspective and don't make a show of herself and prefer not to be put in the spotlight. Teresa's Destiny Number 9 makes her a humanitarian. Six alphabets represent loving, nurturing and responsible personality. Soul Number 11 (vowels) is a master vibration that represents justice and service. Teresa was fascinated by stories of the lives of missionaries and their service to mankind in her childhood and was convinced that she should commit herself to a religious life. Teresa experienced what she later described as "the call within the call" while traveling by train in India. "I was to leave the convent and help the poor while living among them. It was an order. To fail would have been to break the faith". She began her missionary work with the poor and for over 45 years she ministered in her own way to the poor, sick, orphaned, and dying, while guiding the Missionaries of Charity's expansion, first throughout India and then in other countries. Following her death she was beatified by Pope John Paul II and given the title 'Blessed Teresa of Calcutta'.

Gora

Name Number 23

Another great reformer who falls under the vibration of the Ace of Wands is Goparaju Ramachandra Rao popularly known as Gora. He devoted his life to propagating atheism. Throughout the 1940s he worked in the India Independence movement, and after Gandhi's assassination retained his links with leaders of the Gandhian movement, especially Vinoba Bhave. Gora wrote many books, such as Atheism Questions and Answers, An Atheist Around the World, An Atheist with Gandhi, The Need of Atheism, and Positive Atheism. Gora's atheism dictated his campaign to abolish the caste system with its "untouchables," and the idea of "karma" or divine fate. His Atheist Center continues to provide counseling, promotes intercaste and casteless marriages, works to abolish child marriages, provides aid to prostitutes, unwed mothers and vulnerable women, debunks superstitious beliefs by holding firewalking demonstrations and debunking other "miracles," educates against belief in witchcraft and sorcery, promotes sexual

education and family planning and many other reforms.

TWO OF WANDS

A merchant from the top floor of his castle looks out to sea, waiting for his ships to bring him prosperity. A small globe in his right hand indicates that achievement is imminent and he has the whole world "at his fingertips.". A wand in his left hand and the other mounted in reserve shows that he has backup plans that stem from his independent vision. The man is standing at a good vantage point, where he can see the vivid picture of path ahead. An indentation on the parapet is decorated with a lilies and roses diagonally. This indicates a balance between a white lily of thought and the red rose of desire. Empowered decision making and recognition of multiple opportunities is represented in this card. So it is important to get clear about your desires or motivations before choosing the path you will ultimately follow. Best things come to those who have the patience to wait for them, but that doesn't mean to sit idly. Success is imminent through right choices and hard work. Interestingly, a contrasting explanation can be given to the same tarot. A lord overlooking his empire and alternately contemplating a globe reminds us of the restlessness of Alexander to conquer the world that brought him unexpected death. So, beware of being reckless, arrogant, dominating and intolerant as these could bring sudden losses and failures.

Ratan Tata

Name Number 24

Ratan Tata is the present chairman of Tata Group. Ratan Tata was born on 28 December 1937 that makes him a Capricorn who has a style of his own. Self-possessed and intelligent, he has great social skills, including the ability to make anyone feel at home. He takes pride and enjoyment in performing everyday tasks, believing it is through the minor events that character is formed and tested. He generally has a happy outlook.

Ratan Tata, the adopted in the Tata family and is the great-grandson of Tata group founder Jamsetji Tata. He completed the Advanced Management Program at Harvard Business. He turned down a job with IBM and started to work on the shop floor at Tata Steel with other blue- collar employees, shoveling limestone and handling the blast furnace and eventually rose to become the group chairman of the Tata group. As group chairman, he has been responsible for converting "the corporate commonwealth" of different Tata-affiliated companies into a cohesive company. As of 2011, Ratan Tata has an income whose net worth is US $ 970 million. He does not figure in the Forbes' list of Indian millionaires because a large number of the shares (around 65.8%) of Tata Sons, the holding company of the Tata Group, are held by charitable trusts.

THREE OF WANDS

The Tree of Wands is depicted by a calm, majestic personage, with his back turned, looking from a cliff's edge at ships sailing over the sea. From this vantage point, he can see all that lies ahead and is aware of the impending challenges and opportunities. Three wands are planted in the ground, and he leans slightly on one of them. The three Wands surrounding him are firmly planted in the soil symbolize the facets of mind, heart and action, united as ONE, reflecting his commitment to his future plans.

Those who fall under the influence of the Three of Wands possess vision and foresight. They have the ability to see how the present moment fits in with the past and future, and rise above the game to a place of fresh and intuitive perspective to their ventures. These people are courageous and also have good analytical power. This card encourages them to think big. Compare this figure to the Fool who is also on a cliff edge. The Fool steps out in innocence, not realizing he is going to fall to his fate. The person in the Three of Wands is also willing to step out, but with full awareness of what he is doing. His courage is more informed, if less spontaneous. The Three of Wands encourages the natives to move fearlessly into new

Charaka

Name Number 25

Charaka was one of the principal contributors to the ancient art and science of Ayurveda, a system of medicine and lifestyle developed in Ancient India. He lived around 300 BC. His Name Number 25 well as 7 alphabets makes him a visionary with analytical ability and a researcher in medicine without any modern day equipment. According to Charaka's Ayurvedic treatise 'Charaka Samhita', prevention of all types of diseases have a more prominent place than treatment, including restructuring of life style to align with the course of nature and four seasons, which will guarantee complete wellness. These remarks appear obvious today. His treatise contains many such remarks which are held in reverence even today. Some of them are in the fields of physiology, etiology and embryology. Charaka was also the first physician to present the concept of digestion, metabolism and immunity in as early as 300 BC. He is also referred to as the Father of Indian Medicine.

FOUR OF WANDS

T

he Four of Wands is depicted by a couple dancing beneath a welcome wreath, tied between four wands. The canopy of flowers on the four wands is to a wedding ceremony representing a time for celebration, fulfillment and satisfaction at the attainment of a goal. The Four of

Wands also means freedom. Freedom can take many forms, but it always brings with it an exhilarating feeling. In numerology, four symbolizes stability and firm foundations.

Those who fall under the influence of this card enjoy happiness and stability in their life. This card also indicates a sense of harmony and balance. The Four of Wands is one of the most positive cards in the Tarot deck and indicates general good fortune, satisfaction, and fulfillment of the

native's dreams.

Guo Pu

Name Number 26

Guo Pu was a Taoist mystic, geomancer, collector of strange tales, editor of old texts, and erudite commentator. He was a natural historian and a prolific writer who wrote The Book of Burial, an early source of feng shui doctrine. Feng shui is a Chinese system of geomancy believed to use the laws of both infinite intelligence and Earth to help improve one's life by receiving positive energy. Today, feng shui

is practiced not only by the Chinese, but also by Westerners.

FIVE OF WANDS

In the Five of Wands, we see five men of different colors fighting with each other in a rugged field. However, there is no evidence of jaw- breaking, rib-poking or crippling blows to the men in the card. In this sense it connects with the battle of life. The differing colors indicate the difference of opinion and perception among themselves. The Five of Wands shows two types of conflict - outer and inner. The former arises when the world around you is filled with hassles and minor obstacles that slow down your progress and become increasingly difficult to overcome. The latter meaning manifests in times of difficult ethical choices. This card brings restriction, limitation, frustration and annoyance to those who fall under the influence of this number. They may also be prone to accidents, legal disputes and financial problems. In marriage, these people may face domestic struggles in their relationship with their spouse and/or in-laws. At work there may be opposition with your coworkers. There may be challenges and tough competition from rivals in business. These natives will have to work a little harder than usual. In such situations, once again, a clear head will prevail whereas hot-headed personalities get overwhelmed by difficulties. It's important to remember to take the time to process your own feelings. Internal struggles within the natives may be influencing their behavior towards their partners. They should learn to keep the channels of communication open and remember to remain flexible to lead a peaceful life. The natives will always succeed if you can tap the fiery energy for a constructive purpose by co-operating instead of arguing and quarrelling. Compromise if you must, but stand up for your point of view. Refuse to be a victim at the same time; do not lose your cool, even while standing on the hottest coals. Nature is generally harmonious; but human beings bring chaos with their disruptive nature. Learn to be tactful to resolve strife and establish harmony in your life.

Lenin

Name Number 27

Vladimir Ilyich Lenin popularly known as Lenin was a Russian Marxist revolutionary and communist politician who led the October Revolution in 1917. When Lenin was seventeen years old, his sister was arrested and his eldest brother was hanged for participating in an assassination attempt against the Tsar. Those events have contributed to Lenin's radicalization. As leader of the Bolsheviks, he headed the Soviet state during its initial years, as it fought to establish control of Russia in the Russian Civil War and worked to create a socialist economic system. As a politician, Lenin was a persuasive orator. As a political scientist his extensive theoretic and philosophical developments of Marxism produced Marxism-Leninism. In his lifetime, Lenin went through severe mental strains of leading a revolution, governing, and fighting a civil war. He suffered from wounds caused during the assassination attempts on him. In spite of retaining a bullet in his neck, he was working almost ceaselessly, fourteen to sixteen hours daily until his death.

Chapter 18: Personality Number

the personality number is said to reflect your outward personality and show you a bit more about how others perceive you within a short time of getting to know you. It gives insight into the first impressions you give to others and might even come as a bit of a surprise.

As with many other numbers in Numerology, we use your name to calculate this number. The personality number varies a bit however in that you will only use the consonants of your full birth name.

So, what do the numbers have to say about your personality and how you come across? Grab a pen and let's find out.

Write your full birth name across the top of a sheet of paper. Using the chart below, write down the numbers that correspond with only the consonants of your name.

For Example

John Adam Smith would be

JHN DM SMTH

985 44 1424

Source

Next we reduce the numbers down to either a single digit or master number (11, 22, etc).

For the core personality number here, we are going to reduce the whole name all together. Take your numbers from above as follows and add them across.

9 + 8 + 5 + 4 + 4 = 1 + 4 + 2 + 4 = 42 Then we reduce the answer down again

4 + 2 = 6

This means Mr. Smith's personality number is a 6.

Once you have your number determined – read on below to learn a bit about what your number says about you.

Personality Number 1

This personality comes across as confident, smart, and highly independent. This is a natural leader who tends to dominate or will naturally rise to the forefront of any group. One people are also prone to being very distinctive individuals who don't mind standing out in the crowd. They leave a very strong impress on on those they encounter and can sometimes come across as aloof and possibly even a bit conceited to others if they don't learn to share the floor.

Personality Number 2

This is your peacekeeper, the one who weighs both sides of every story before making a decision. Personality wise, he/she may seem to be open and naturally curious or inquisitive. They don't just want to know what you think about something, but why you think that way.

Those with this number are often seen as trustworthy due to their well-rounded nature and tendency to not make snap judgments. At times, two's can be indecisive which may cause them to appear to lack confidence. Overall Two people come across as well-balanced however, displaying a "middle road" approach to life.

Personality Number 3

People with a 3 personality number are natural communicators with an outstanding knack for expression in many forms. They can express complex concepts and ideas articulately, yet in a manner that is easy for everyone to understand. The three person is open to opportunities and they tend to be optimistic or to at least look for something to glean from challenges in life. 3 people are great story tellers and have a flare for being expressive (talking with hand gestures for example). Sometimes their flare for the dramatic can be seen as a bit over the top, but always entertaining.

Personality Number 4

This person is often seen as very serious and dedicated, stoic and with a good "poker face". This personality doesn't wear his/her heart on the sleeve in the least, but they don't seem disconnected or aloof either. Cool as a cucumber and very aware, these are the personalities you would want to be around in the event of a crisis or emergency. Four people are seen as reliable, stable and sometimes are prone to being too predictable. Spontaneous behaviors are very uncharacteristic of a four. This is a hard worker who makes a "good neighbor" in most cases.

Personality Number 5

Five people tend to take charge also, but they love a group dynamic. These are the types who are the first to take the dance floor, but they also want to pull others in and break the ice. They are socially inclined, have leadership ability or initiative and they also tend to love exploration and travel. Five people are not always the most reliable when it comes to being places on time or doing things on a strict schedule. They can come across as a tad flaky, but as having their hearts in the right place.

Personality Number 6

This personality is the maternal/paternal sort, the caretaker and one who wants to nurture others and provide comfort. Six people are natural cheerleaders and love to see others succeed. They get along with a variety of people, work hard to avoid conflict and will work diligently to reach compromises with others. They thrive best in a "family" unit and will strive to bring that kind of bonding into other areas of life. They are usually great people to work with for that reason - the real "team players".

Personality Number 7

This personality tends to quiet, reflective and often quite introverted. The 7 person is very self-aware, but also acutely in tune to the emotions of others. With these people still waters run deep and they tend to be a bit socially awkward in large groups, but are mesmerizing in one on one conversations or in small groups of trusted individuals. They are naturally drawn to psychology, philosophy and exploring the deeper meaning of life and human nature. Seven people can be difficult to get to know, but once you get through to them, they are very loyal and trustworthy people.

Personality Number 8

Eight people are competitive, ambitious, dynamic and hard working. People with this number are always pushing themselves to reach higher and their determination and energy can become contagious to others around them – even if it happens to be because you feel like a shrinking violet in their presence. Eight people are good at visualizing things and making them happen. They set their minds to things and are unstoppable. They appear confident, lucky and sometimes overly enthusiastic to others.

Personality Number 9

This personality is a natural charmer who tends to be idealistic and optimistic. Nine people are very conscientious people who put equal value on all people. A nine individual is not someone who would look down on others who have a different lot in life, they would see a homeless person as being just as valuable as anyone else, whereas many others would rush to judgment. This fairness and conscientious nature of the 9 person sometimes draws them to be leaders, particularly in humanitarian capacities. People gravitate towards this person's positivity and altruistic nature. At times, they can seem a bit "preachy" or so idealistic that they deny certain realities.

Personality Number 11

This master number has the leadership capacity of the 1, but usually with less ego or "my first" kind of energy. 11 people are valued and looked up to for their wisdom. A properly balanced personality with a master number will be one of those people who seem "larger than life" but in a good way – not a "look at me" kind of fashion. Eleven people value themselves and treat themselves with respect and lead by example, encouraging those same traits in others. Eleven people believe in the power of human greatness and hold themselves and others accountable for their own choices in life, but in a merciful, empowering way.

Personality Number 22

This personality number is one who is very well balanced indeed. They will be both artistic and analytical for example. They can be practical and hard-working, but will balance that exceptionally well with personal interests and hobbies. They are the "work hard play hard" types. They also strive to create harmony in their lives and crave consistency. This strong personality is capable of great things due to their high levels of creative talents and discipline.

Conclusion

☐ Check the numbers and alphabets in the introduction chapter and find your name digits or sum accordingly. If not lucky, change letters or names to good numbers as said in above chapters as per your date of birth.

☐ Though there are many alternate belief systems exist in the world, numerology is the key for every success as letters and associated numbers are two eyes of life.

☐ If a person born in lucky day, but his name is unlucky then everything will be in vain in life.

☐ Choosing name is a mandatory project in life that we have to do without fail.

☐ Date of marriage, date of joining office/work, date of opening a company or shop etc must be in lucky day than auspicious day!

☐ After changing the name, you must write minimum 32 times daily in a note book daily or weekly 4 or 5 day at least. Then only it will create good vibration and luck for the newly set number.

☐ If there is unlucky name from childhood, at any time you can change your name. It will not harm if properly chosen. Age doesn't matter.

☐ As people name or organization name or company name etc, the Place/ Country name also matters a lot. Example: Switzerland = 41, USA = 10, India = 12, Brazil = 16

etc.

☐ Even if you suffer a lot with bad start date or birth date or bad name number, you can change at any age and start writing the same daily 32 times will give positive results one by one within three months.

☐ Only numbers 5, 6 and few lucky numbers under 1, 3 & 9 are most powerful lucky numbers which will help the people to move up and rule with prosperity, health, abundance & long life.

☐ Apply numerology practically than the theoretical concepts.

☐ For any assistance or guidance in numerology/ astrology, please visit

www.ingramcontent.com/pod-product-compliance
Lightning Source LLC
Chambersburg PA
CBHW072002070526
44583CB00015B/1304